Laughing!
THE **HA** THAT HEALS

 BY: THELMA SHIRLEY-TAYLOR

LAUGH AGAIN **"The Ha That Heals"**
Copyright 2012 By Thelma ShirleyTaylor

Published in the U.S. By:
SPAA PUBLICATIONS
P.O. Box 22
Park Forest, IL 60466
(708) 785 7371
Website: www.thespaa.org
Email: national@thespaa.org

All rights reserved. No part of this book may be used or reproduced by any means, graphic, electronic, or mechanical, including photocopying, recording, taping or by any information storage retrieval; system without the written permission of the author except in the case of brief quotations embodied in critical articles and reviews.

Graphic Illustrations: Sylvia Westbrook

Cover Design By: Rachel Gadson

Edited By: Kelly Small

ISBN: 987-0-9826141-7-4

Printed in the United States of America

LAUGH AGAIN; "The HA THAT HEALS"

TABLE OF CONTENTS

FORWARD:	Hermene Hartman, Publisher N'Digo	2
PREFACE:	Dr. Michael V. Wilkins, Founder SPAA	6
DEDICATION/ACKNOWLEDGMENTS:		8
MESSAGE TO THE READERS:		10
INTRODUCTION:		12

PART 1: THE SCIENCE OF LAUGHTER:

We're Changing	15
Comedy The Remedy	33
Practice Safe Stress	43
Parenting With Humor & Laughter	51
The Cannon Twins Arrive	55
Rev. James Ford, "The Storyteller"	68
A Teacher's Secret Use of Humor	73
Dr. Oprah Winfrey: Everybody Gets A Car	86
Christian Funny Men & Women	101
The Clown Prince Of Physicians	105
Betty White: The Last Golden Girl	118
Comedians: Sinbad and Steve Harvey	122
The World Still Loves Lucy	125

PART II WHERE THE JOKES ARE:

Chapter i: The Kidz Korner	132
Chapter II: Adult Jokes	162
Chapter III: Church Jokes	181
Chapter IV: Corporate Humor	198
Chapter V: Sizzling Seniors	219

FORWARD

THE SCIENCE OF THE LAUGH

By Hermene Hartman, Publisher, N'Digo Magapaper

We all appreciate humor. There is nothing like a good laugh from a giggle to a bellyache. Everyone appreciates a good joke or an amusing story. Every good speech from the president to the preacher and teacher; from corporate executive to the motivational speaker uses a joke to make a point or gain pause. Some professional speechwriters hire jokesters to assist. The lighter side makes the speech sparkle as it appeals to the commonality of listeners.

Great comedians like Bob Hope, Don Rickles, Johnny Carson, Bill Cosby, Richard Pryor, Robin Williams, Steve Harvey, Phyllis Diller, Lucille Ball and Joan Rivers are laugh masters. They make us take a look at ourselves in daily living and chuckle at life situations. Their situations might range from romance, marriage to housework to raising children. These funny people can make the darndest things simple and funny and turn the complex and even grave issues to comical. All of them have made storytelling an art form.

Thelma Shirley Taylor has taken a look at hilarity in a variety of ways. She has examined the power of laughter from a doctor's and patient's view, concluding with testimony that laughter is good for you and has proven health benefits. She provides us with examples from universal daily living experiences from the simplicity of the child's point of view, to the spiritual connection, no matter religion.

Laugh Again has a spiritual component. The last few years have been challenging with technology innovations that have transformed industries, economic downturn causing massive unemployment and home foreclosures. Bankruptcies have been filed at a historic rate. We have seen debating politicians become the butt of the jokes on late night TV as they provided new characters for Saturday Night Live.

Many people are depressed with attitudes of the downtrodden. The social climate has been gloomy. Thelma is a student of truth and knows the power of thinking and that thinking alone can change your life. It is from this premise that she searched a way to make people take laughter seriously, so that they could change their attitudes and spiritual directions. She has sought to bring uplift to their situations.

In this book she talks about the healing power of laughter. She provides examples, documentation and experiences that jolt a reality check. One of the more powerful examples is the patient who was given a short time to live and gathered funny videos and he and his wife watched them daily. He outlived his doctor's prognosis. He was determined not to die sad but happy. Laughter provides a healing power. The dying man prolonged his life because he laughed. A great way to invite people to a party is to head the list with those who make you laugh.

The Ha That Heals lightens your load. She gives us prescription for laughter and this book is your guide to its benefit and how it impacts our lives. You are better off laughing than not.

It was a very good year, as Thelma got serious with her writing, collecting jokes and humorous tales. She often shared them with her email list; of which I was included. I am a radio commentator on Clear Channel in Chicago on weekdays, providing social comment for *Views from the Heart.* Often I have used her humorous tales for the audiences to make them smile and laugh. I am particularly fond of those about the honesty of children and the wisdom of the elderly. They provide powerful life messages.

To live a successful life is to laugh often. Have you ever noticed people who laugh appear happier and more successful than those who don't? Every day you should laugh, the more the better. Laughter is a part of life's magic and you are enriched if you do so. **Laugh Again: The Ha That Heals** is for everyone. Enjoy. Laugh.

PREFACE

By Dr. Michael V. Wilkins, Sr. (Founder of SPAA)

Sometime ago, I met *Thelma Shirley Taylor*, a vibrant and feisty lady who attended and joined the *SPAA (Speakers, Publishers and Authors Association*.). She quickly pulled me aside to tell me that she was working on a book and asked if I would help. I agreed and met with her. To my surprise, I discovered that she had hundreds of pages of her writings scattered throughout various folders, on her computer, on tables, the floor and in file cabinets. My first thought was, "We can do this!" (Perhaps I was trying to convince myself as much as encourage Thelma.) But when she stood in the middle of her living room, in the exact spot where she had asked God to give her something to do to help all the suffering people in the world, *"something that would lift their spirits"*, I knew that this would be one of the most exciting projects that I have ever been involved with. I have personally written over 15 books and published literally hundreds for others, but there are only a few that came even close to having the positive effects of '**LAUGH AGAIN**'.

I encourage each of you to share your enjoyment with others. What better gift to give to someone who seems to always be angry, upset or depressed, than a book of God inspired laughter.

As a doctor, pastor and professional consultant, my prescription to all of you is this delightful book, designed to encourage, inspire and entertain...especially those of you who may be depressed, adversely affected by the economic times, or those of you who remember laughter and simply want to *LAUGH AGAIN*. I invite all of you to have a dose of "**LAUGH AGAIN: The "Ha That Heals"**. I thank God for Thelma and her unselfish obedience, sacrifice and commitment to share with the world what God have given her; the powerful and wonderful medicine of the healing power of humor.

DEDICATION

This labor of love and laughter is dedicated to my wonderful patient husband, Fred, who took over all of our household duties during the two years I spent researching and writing this book. Thanks Babe. I couldn't have done it without you.

ACKNOWLEDGMENTS

Proving the One Power

With the deepest of appreciation, I thank some of the best friends and family members on the planet for sharing their jokes, quotes and funny stories. Their support shows up in Chapters I-V. I call them my Joyologists. Love to "Lil Sis" Marilyn Ward (New Jersey); Delores Williams My Dr. of Humor (Houston, TX); My songstress, Niecy Randall (Tucson, AZ) and loving godchildren Sylvia and Jim McCallister (Phoenix, AZ) who faithfully emailed some of the wittiest stories. Sadly, we lost Jim recently during the final pages of my book. I miss him. My wonderful niece Sheryl Jerman (Austin TX) and my first cousin Pat Reilly (Bartlesville, OK) also sent some awesome data between their grand mothering.

And, my only godson, Eric Keyes, II (Lynwood, IL) who was a regular contributor. Another one of my special daughters, Tonya Clemons Reese (Los Angeles, CA) telephoned me nearly every day checking on my progress and health. Love you all.

Mama T.

MESSAGE TO THE READERS

Today is not just another day. It is a GIFT of more time. Thankfulness should be your response. Cultivate happy thoughts by starting to smile, chuckle, giggle or indulge in a big, bold, bodacious laugh. Think about your next 24 hours as if it were your first and/or the last day. Isn't it incredible what is being offered to you – moment to moment. Can you put a value on this gift?

Now, open your eyes and see your wonderful world of opportunities. Open your heart and you will become a blessing to others by merely smiling at the people in and around your space. Do you realize you have been given the ability to just 'be', 'see', and to 'speak' along with so many other gifts. Experience the overflowing joy you can wrap your mind around. This, then, will be a GREAT Day.

So often you hear that laughter is the best medicine. In your hands you hold the laugh maker. So why not LAUGH AGAIN, AND AGAIN. It is, you know, the 'HA THAT HEALS'. Enjoy.

Thelma Shirley-Taylor

THE MISSION OF LAUGH AGAIN

This publication was written to demonstrate one of God's greatest gifts, the healing power of humor therapy. The amazing outcome of this blessed command is great health, peace, happiness, an uncluttered mind by the magical use of God's positive energy.

INTRODUCTION

"After God created the world, he created man and woman. Then, to keep the whole thing from collapsing, he created humor."
               Ernie Hobercht

Welcome to your new companion, "LAUGH AGAIN: The 'HA' THAT HEALS". You will find a treasure trove of amusing, entertaining, inspirational jokes and stories along with scientific, therapeutic and medical research on the healing properties of this powerful and amazing intervention.

Like prescription pills, laughter and humor heals without side effects. It can eradicate depression, release anger and pain, chase away loneliness and sadness, as well as many other counterproductive challenges threatening your life experience.

Because we are living possibly in the most stressful and unstable cycle of time on this planet, mankind hungers for every kind of distraction and diversion available in his constant effort to survive.

This search is by no means new. In the Middle Ages, kings, monarchs and rulers sought the help of entertainers to quiet the anger, frustration and melancholy, festering in their kingdoms and relief from their governmental pressures. The benefit of humor therapy was acknowledged as far back as the Book of Proverbs in the Old Testament of the Bible, which contains verses like, "*A cheerful heart is good medicine, but a downcast spirit dries up the bones.*" (Proverbs 17:22).

Historians report that King Solomon gave us one of the earliest accounts of the healing spirit of merriment. In the 1300's, French surgeon Henri De Mondeville wrote, "Let the surgeon take care to regulate the whole regimen of the patient's life for joy and happiness, allowing his relatives and special friends to cheer him and by having someone tell him incredibly funny jokes." Mondeville told jokes to his patients in the recovery room.

During the 1600's, educator Richard Mulcater recommended laughter for even those suffering from head colds. Martin Luther used a form of humor therapy as part of his pastoral counseling of depressed people. He advised them not to isolate themselves but to interact with friends who could joke and make them laugh. Many of Luther's own letters to other people included playful and humorous remarks.

Modern humor therapy dates from the 1930's when clowns were brought into hospitals to cheer up children hospitalized with polio.

The love of comedy has always been inherent in most cultures. Today's laughmakers are descendants of early harlequins, clowns and court jesters. Like their historic counterparts, the modern day crop of comics are more irreverent, inventive and uncommonly gifted. Comedy is dominating the 21st century's entertainment arena. It has become a multi-billion dollar industry and is still expanding.

A great number of clinical studies helped verify the healing art of humor that heals man's mind and body without drugs. In general, laughter improves the physical, mental, emotional and spiritual health of the body. A happy state of mind appears to release tension in the diaphragm and relieve pressure on the liver and other internal organs. It stimulates the immune system, reduces stress and helps balance the body's natural energy fields, or auras. People who have developed a strong sense of humor, exhibit more control over their lives.

WE'RE CHANGING

The enlightening information we have collected from some of the most unlikely sources, will stimulate your spirit as it endorses the science of it. Science suggests that our world is the mirror of our beliefs, however, whatever we once believed, is about to change.

Scientist Gregg Braden wrote in his recent book Fractal Time, "We are living the completion of a 5,125 year cycle of time…a world age calculated by the ancient Mayans which would end with the winter solstice on December 23, 2012." He hastens to tell us, *"Don't define this completion as the end of the world. A new cycle will provide us with a planet change filled with great opportunities."* Dr. Arthur Wang Pinero believes *"The future is only the past again, entered through another gate"*.

Hive Yong Jang, author of the Gaia Project 2012, says, "Human beings have the unseasoned experience of losing everything they think they own, thus they will learn the true joy of being free of the burdens of their possessions. When we realize that we do not own anything in this material world, all of our fears and anxieties will disappear." Jang adds. "The earth's great change is in progress.

The change that has been promised in song, sermon and verse all through the 20th century is here. Be patient, people, and prepare to learn the new lessons. We're heading for a rebirth to a higher dimension. This is a blessing not a catastrophe. What is the purpose? It is for each person to expand in consciousness. Our powers will return magnified, intensified and heightened. Then we will know the true joy, health and happiness.

> *"Don't worry about the world coming to an end today.*
> *It is already tomorrow in Australia."*
> Charles M. Schultz

"Thou Shall Laugh"

THE SCIENCE OF LAUGHTER

Did you know that laughter is your birthright? It is a natural part of life that is innate, and believe it or not, you were born with your giggles. Do you remember hearing some parents say about their infant's grins, giggles, smiling noises, *"Oh, it's just a little gas."* Not true. Laughter exists on its own merit. It is a unique resonance to your joy.

Kristi Helvig, license psychologist believes that laughter helps increase physical health. She says laughing actually causes a physical reaction that can improve our physical and mental state. As you will find throughout the book, you do not have to "get the joke, hear a story or decipher a code in order to laugh. Laughter is a gift and it is a tool. It is energy that comes to our aid whenever we choose to use it.

Because cheerfulness is so infectious, others will immediately react. When you laugh, you spread joy just by merely being your happy self.

When you apply gaiety to your life, you are also providing healing to your mind, body and spirit. Think of humor as the brain waves jumpstarting your pleasure zones. Read something amusing, listen to funny audiobooks, reflect on your favorite jokes, and spend a few minutes laughing out loud...on your way to work, preparing for a job interview, or taking a test. It's a safe, healthy and pleasurable activity and it works.

Consider the last time you laughed until your stomach hurt. You probably felt pretty good, even after you stopped laughing. Just as anxiety releases stress hormones, such as cortisol and epinephrine (adrenalin), laughing has been found to decrease these same receptors as morphine which can produce the feeling of relaxation and a heightened mood. Levels of Dopamine Serotonin and Norepinephrine are altered as well. Researchers then wondered what the physical changes that take place in the rate of breathing, in blood pressure and the increase of our heart rates. What they found was a combination of physical changes in the body that occurred with laughter. Each one of these changes by itself produced small effects but together was synergistic in producing these stress relieving and mood altering results.

It was interesting to note that spontaneous laughing was far better than self-produced laughter.

LAUGHTER IS INTOXICATING

Laughing is a powerful antidote. Nothing works faster or more dependably to bring the mind and body back in balance than a good satisfying laugh. It is found to lower blood pressure, reduce stress hormones, increase muscle flexion and boost immune function. Humor lightens your burdens, inspires hope, connects you to others and keeps you grounded, focused and alert.

THERE IS POWER IN HA, HA, HA

With so much power available to heal and renew the body, the ability to laugh easily and frequently is a tremendous resource for surmounting problems, enhancing relationships and supporting both physical and emotional health.

Just think, a big hearty Ha, Ha, Ha and you will immediately begin to feel better and good feelings remain with your long after the merriment subsides.

HOW TO BE YOUR HAPPIEST

Researchers have long recognized that your state of mind can be effectively influenced and controlled by your choice of moods. Choose to be happy with the help of humor, laughter, and with friends with lighthearted personalities. Science is buttressing laughter's impressive therapeutic properties. According to a growing number of enthusiastic adherents, laughter has the potential to cure disease, kill pain and get the body back in shape.

While the medical and pharmaceutical community charges millions of dollars for drugs and compounds that they call "mood products", they come with many side effects. The most obvious way to be your happiest is simply utilize the blessings of laughter and this is absolutely free. Begin your therapy now. It's the "Ha! That Heals."

GOING CRAZY CAN BE FUNNY

David Granirer and other comics create and perform original material dealing with their mental health journey. Granirer, a counselor, stand-up comic, and the author of The Happy Neurotic: How Fear and Angst Can Lead To Happiness and Success. He is also the creator of STAND UP FOR MENTAL HEALTH (SMH).

Granirer teaches stand-up comedy to people with mental illness as a way of building their confidence and fighting public stigma, prejudice and discrimination. "Our shows look at the lighter side of taking meds, seeing counselors, getting diagnosed and surviving the mental health system. We perform at conferences, treatment centers and psych wards in partnership with numerous mental health groups." SMH performs in prisons and military bases, universities and college campuses as well as government, corporate and community fundraising forums. Most importantly, they perform for the general public across Canada and the United States.

David, who has depression, says, "If you have bipolar disorder, depression, schizophrenia, obsessive compulsive disorder, post-traumatic stress disorder or mental health diagnosis, you're a perfect fit for the program."

We use comedy to give consumers a powerful voice and help reduce the stigma and discrimination around mental illness, he adds.

Pat Hayes, executive director for the Vancouver-based SMH says "one hundred percent of us will deal with mental illness in our lives. Data shows that 15 percent of university students will be diagnosed with a mental illness issues alone. Mental Health is an integral part of your overall health and well-being. Students need to care for their minds the way they care for their bodies, and not be embarrassed to seek help.

Although no official training or certification is required, there are a few institutions that teach humor therapy. Further information is available from the American Association For Therapeutic Humor.

"War does not determine who is right…
Only who is left.
Anonymous

HOW DOES LAUGHTER START?

It usually begins with a little smile and sometimes, it ends with a tear. When you hear... really HEAR that insuperable 'crasher', the tsunami of all side-splitting jokes, pay attention to your own reaction and observe someone else's. Did it feel something like this?

Your eyes snap wide open and then squints; your head repositions itself, robotic-like; your face fractures into a thousand little lines and grins; and then an indiscernible sound begins to rumble deep inside the pit of your stomach...like a roller-coaster; it roars through your body, screaming to get out of your mouth which has flung itself wide open to allow this JOY to escape. With that good kind of pain and happy relief, you ENJOY! Then comes the big exhale, followed by a soft smile and whimper as you wipe away a tiny tear. You salute the laughmaker with a kind of satisfaction that only laughter can bring. Sitting there with your waning grin in anticipation, you readjust; perk your ears, as you get ready to LAUGH AGAIN.

THE MECHANICS OF BLISS

Jennifer Margulis writes in The State of the Smile, "That which goes from ear to ear, isn't as simple as it appears." So much more than a pair of upturned lips, the smile is one of the most scientifically studied human facial expressions. She says scientists in fields from biology to anthropology to computer science, sheds a lot of light on "The Happy Face". Margulis believes:

Smiles exert subliminal powers

There are three degrees of happiness

There are two types of smiles (genuine and fake)

To spot a faker, check the eyes

Smiles have accents...United States-mouths...Japan the eyes

Peoples with big grins live longer

THERE'S SOMETHING ABOUT YOUR SMILE

Is there actually something about jokes and the resulting laughter that can change our health in a beneficial way? What is it about laughter that we love so much? Why are comedies so popular? Why is there such a thing as 'comic relief' and why is it so effective... even in the most serious of plays and dramas?

Well you won't be surprised to find that scientists have learned that there is actually something about laughter that affects us more profoundly than we think. Basically there is good evidence now that laughter produced by jokes can change the chemical milieu that moves through our bodies on a second to second basis. Researchers then wondered what action was producing these changes. Was it smiling, or the physical changes that take place in the rate of breathing, in blood pressure and the increase of our heart rates? What they found was a combination of physical changes in the body that occur with laughter.

MAKE HAPPY DAYS

The miraculous power of laughter creates miracles. John Milton said that happiness allows us to encounter everyday epiphanies...those moments of awe that change how we experience life. A daily practice, a planned laughter session, as you might with working out at the gym will shift our attitudes, lifting us to a place of hope and joy...and an inner dance will unfold. Here are some ways to start:

...SMILE

Pioneers in laugh therapy find It's possible to laugh without even experiencing a funny event. The same holds true when you look at someone or see something even mildly amusing. Smile. Practice until you can do it effortlessly.

...COUNT YOUR BLESSINGS

Literally, make a list. The simple act of considering the good things in your life will distance you from the negative thoughts that are barriers to humor and merriment. Lee Iacocca said, *"The discipline of writing something down, is the first step towards making it happen."*

...SPEND TIME WITH PLAYFUL PEOPLE

These are people who laugh easily, both as themselves and at life's absurdities, and who routinely find the humor in everyday events. Their playful point of view and laughter are contagious.

Anyone can join the laughter movement. All it takes is a willingness to risk some loss of control. The timid may start with a few shy giggles; The courageous may jump in with a deep belly laugh; A sense of humor is not required...there is more than enough 'stress' to go around. All we have to do is believe...let go...clap your hands and laughter will live again. And so will we. (Enda Junkins).

"Angels fly because they take themselves lightly.

G.K. Chesteron

WHAT A GOOD LAUGH FEELS LIKE

"Nothing feeds the soul like a great laugh. Not that chuckle you save for your boss, and "bougie" company, but a good gutbuster that causes you to blow liquid through your nose, bend over because you can't stand up straight, hold your sides and work your tear ducts overtime." Now, visualize that!!!

Terry Glover

More than just a respite from sadness and pain, laughter provides the courage and strength to find new sources of meaning and hope. Even in the most difficult times, a laugh or even simply a smile can go a long way toward making you feel relaxed and at ease.

LAUGHTER IS LIKE SPEAKING IN TONGUES

"Whether overheard in a crowded restaurant, punctuating the enthusiastic chatter of friends, or as the noisy guffaws on a TV Sound track, laughter is a fundamental part of everyday life. It is so common that we forget how strange and important it is. Indeed, laughter is "speaking in tongues" in which we're moved not by religious fervor, but by an unconscious response to social and linguistic uses.

Stripped of its variation and nuance, laughter is a regular series of short vowel-like syllables usually transcribed as "ha-ha, ho-ho or hee-hee." These syllables are part of the universal human vocabulary, produced and recognized by people of all cultures," says scientist Robert Provine.

THE SOUND OF JOY

The sound of roaring laughter is far more transmittable than any cough, sniffle or sneeze. When laughter is shared, it binds people together and increases happiness and intimacy. In the domino effect of joy and amusement, laughter also triggers healthy physical changes in the body. These miraculous "pain lifters" strengthens our immune system.

Robert Provine writes "given the universality of the sound, our ignorance about the purpose and meaning of laughter is remarkable. We somehow laugh at just the right times, without consciously knowing why we do it. Most people think of laughter as a simple response to comedy, or a cathartic mood changer." Instead, after 10 years of research on this little studied topic, Provine concluded that laughter is primarily a social vocalization that unites people.

It is a hidden language we all speak. In his book LAUGHTER, he adds "Laughter has been hiding in plain sight."

WHAT ACTUARIES SAY

Laughter is just one of the obvious feel-good human qualities that is suddenly seen by science to be making a difference to human health and outlook. Hugging, singing, smiling and dancing, the fundamentals of human joy, bolstered by hard science, may be powerful, non-cost therapies in themselves. Dr. Charmaine Griffiths, spokesperson for the British Heart Foundation, stated that scientists are increasingly interested in the possibility that positive emotions can be good for your health.

Even AIG, an American Insurance Company is now running ads on U.S. network TV claiming "Laughing will add eight years to your life. A study by the University of North Carolina published in 2005 says women who are hugged regularly appear to have a lower risk of heart disease. A University of Maryland study shows regular laughter improves blood circulation and may protect against heart attack.

Psychiatrist Joseph Richman's study of depressed and suicidal senior citizens showed laughter had a significant curative affect. A 2001 University of California study reported members of a choir showed significantly increased levels of immunity-building proteins just prior to performance and even more dramatically afterward. Clinical psychologist Dan Johnston says that simply smiling for no particular reason can have positive effect on health and attitude. What these have in common is they're all obvious and none require a prescription.

A recent study says that antidepressant drugs don't work. It revealed that in most cases, expensive drugs like Prozac are no more effective than a placebo. What wasn't mentioned was that placebos can be shockingly effective. If people believe they are taking something that will help their condition, they often improve. But perhaps the most intriguing recent laughter breakthrough involves humor. Common misread of Norman Cousin's experience credits him with the discovery that "humor is healthy". Few would argue that having a sense of humor is a healthy thing, but it wasn't humor or positive thinking that saved Cousins, he believed it was laughter. There is a critical distinction.

A man who was coping with chronic kidney failure made an unintentional study of deathbed preoccupations. "One of the main things people remember as they die," he said, "is the great laughs they shared with people."

Those who bring sunshine into the lives of others cannot keep it from themselves.

J.M. Barrie.

COMEDY...THE REMEDY

THE MIRACULOUS POWER OF LAUGHTER

"THE AMAZING NORMAN COUSINS STORY"

In 1964, Norman Cousins, the respected editor of the Saturday Review had been given six months to live. He's been diagnosed with a crippling, life-threatening 'ankylosing spondylitis, the painful degenerative disease of the spine'. Cousins was in constant agony and quickly succumbing to paralysis. The doctors speculated that his chance of survival was approximately 1 in 500. Since drugs were not working, he and his wife gathered up lots of funny videos and dvds by stand-up comedians, including the physical comedies of Laurel and Hardy and The Marx Brothers and he read jokes, jokes and more jokes. The Cousins' secluded themselves in a hotel for three months.

What Cousins found was that when he laughed heartily, he was able to stimulate chemicals in his body that allowed him several hours of pain-free sleep. When the pain returned, he would simply turn the projector back on and the laughter would reinduce sleep again.

Despite intense pain and discomfort, Cousins made a point of laughing so hard that his stomach hurt but this unquenchable laughter never failed to produce a strong reduction in his feelings of pain. Cousins had a strong will to live and knew if he focused on love and faith, he could generate positive emotions.

Cousins died in 1990 at the age of 75. His ideas and research helped launch the 'laughter movement and the positive psychology movement.'

Twenty five years ago, C.K. Chesterton wrote, "I am all in favor of laughing. It has something in common with the ancient winds of faith and inspiration. It unfreezes pride and unwinds secrecy; it makes people forget themselves in the presence of something greater than themselves…something as common as a joke that they cannot resist."

"Researchers found that 100 laughs equal 10 minutes on a rowing machine."

THE POWER CONTINUES

There have been many Norman Cousins type success stories during the past forty-seven years. However, it is the Cousins movie "Anatomy of An Illness" released in 1979 and the Seth Rogan's Cancer film 50/50 released in 2011 that demonstrates the healing power of humor.

50/50 is a warm and continually funny look at the illness that proves how laughter and humor can heal. Will Reisner is now more than five years cancer-free. The comedian-actor says that he's never felt better in his life.

HEAL THYSELF

In the popular book THE SECRET, a personal story of Cathy Goodman, proved once again that the power of laughter and humor healed her breast cancer within three months. Once diagnosed, Cathy followed Dr. Norman Cousins regimen of non-stop, side splitting comedy and hilarious cartoons, so that the real disease of stress was unable to penetrate her mind.

One of THE SECRET's contributing doctors, Bob Proctor says, "Disease cannot live in a body that's in a healthy emotional state." He said the body is casting off millions of cells every second and it's also creating millions of new cells at the same time. In fact, Dr. John Hagelin said, "Part of our bodies are literally replaced every day. Other parts take a few months, while other parts, a couple a years." Within seven years, we each have a brand new physical body." Dr. Hagelin said, "Remove physiological stress from the body and the body does what it was designed to do. It heals itself."

Dr. David Felton, University of Rochester, School of Medicine teaches, "We can no longer pretend that the patient's perceptions don't matter and we cannot pretend that healing is something doctors do to a patient. Your mind is in every cell of your body. Therefore your own "thought's create your reality."

NEUROSCIENCE CONFIRMS: Our bodies respond to social connections. There is much we don't know about neurological underpinnings of laughter, including why laughing feels so good.

One recent study detected evidence that stimulating the nucleus accumbens, one of the brain's pleasure centers, triggers laughter. Some anecdotal and clinical evidence suggests that laughing makes you healthier by suppressing stress hormones and elevating immune system antibodies.

If you think of laughter as being basically synonymous with the detection of humor, the laughing-makes-you-healthier premise seems bizarre. Why would natural selection make your immune system respond to jokes? Dr. Robert Provine helped solve the mystery. He and his staff studied over 1200 natural occurrences of laughter, and found that our bodies aren't responding to punch lines, they are responding to social connection. And even if we don't yet understand the neurological basis of the pleasure that laughing brings us, it makes sense that we should seek out the connectedness of infectious laughter. We are social animals, after all. And if that laughter often involves some pretty childish behavior, so be it.

RESEARCHERS CALCULATE...

Using the powerful tool of mind, we can literally create a reality that mimics our innermost dreams and aspirations. The mind simply gives equal energy to any thought with focus...interpreting that focus as a desire of intent. Happier thoughts lead to essentially a happier biochemistry and a healthier body.

THE MIGHTY FORCE OF DESIRE

Burt Goldman, known as *The American Monk*, reinforces in his latest book *The Power of Self Mind Control,* how desire has degrees of strength. To illustrate this, he tells the story of a disciple who went to his guru and asked "Master, how do I achieve enlightenment?" The wise old guru directed the disciple to the bank of the Ganges River and had him kneel with his head over the water. Then the guru put his hand on the young man's neck and pushed his head below the surface of the water. After a minute and a half, the young disciple was frantic.

He pulled and heaved and flailed his arms, but the grip was like iron. He could not get his head back out of the water. After two minutes, when it seemed as though his lungs would burst, the guru released his grip.

The young man's head jerked out of the water and took great gulps of air into his tortured lungs. The guru smiled. "Tell me", he gently asked, "what was your greatest desire just then?" "To breath." The young disciple stated emphatically. "Ah", the guru said. "When you desire enlightenment to that degree, it shall be yours."

NOW THIS SHOULD MAKE YOU HAPPY

Let's enter the fascinating world of "Knowing" by Jerry and Esther Hicks.

This dynamic duo's world renown book *ASK AND IT IS GIVEN* teaches how to manifest your desires so that you can live a joyous and fulfilling life. In order to receive the instructions, your mind must be clear and clutter-free. Relax and feel!

CLEARING CLUTTER FOR CLARITY

Imagine yourself in an environment of immense order. See the space you live in completely organized and clean. You know where all of your possessions are, and you feel absolutely comfortable. Now enjoy that wonderful feeling of relief.

Every morning as you prepare for meditations, clear the mental and emotional clutter from your mind. Go on a rampage of appreciation. Smile, pray and thank your father, God, for the best day of your life.

"Every time you praise something, everything you feel good about something, you are telling the universe, "More of this please." Stay in that state of appreciation and ALL GOOD THINGS WILL FLOW TO YOU."

And now you're ready to listen and learn how to build your 'Castle.' According to Jerry and Esther, it is just as easy to create a castle as it is to create a button... it is only a matter of whether you are focused on a castle or a button. The trick is...how you are using your energy.

You must make your focus the object of attention. It is summoning the Life Force and the feeling of the Life Force which is what life is all about.

What the authors are saying is rather than visualizing the acquisition of a button, why not create a very positive current of financial abundance, or your best health, happiest relationship, why not create the ability to give people opportunities, jobs, college degrees etc. What better way could anyone spend money than by putting it back into the economy so more people benefit and more people share the good life.

FOCUS – PERCEIVE – CREATE

The Hicks asked their spirit guide Abraham to explain what our role is here on this planet. "Your role is to utilize energy. That is why you exist. You are an energy-flowing-being. You're a Focuser, a Perceiver, you are a Creator and there is nothing worse in all the universe than to come forth into the environment, where desire is easily born, and NOT allow energy to flow to your Desire. That is truly squandering life.

The authors explain, there is no high or low work, only opportunities to focus on." You can feel as fulfilled and satisfied in any task, for you are on the leading edge of thought and source is flowing through you, no matter what your endeavor. Be joyful.

Everything about this physical manifestational experience is spiritual. It is all the end product of spirit. You have nothing to prove. Just be the 'spiritual you' that you are. You have the power. To create, create, create!

The famed Tony Robbins explains, "There is a consistent path to success." He says you will need to:

- Define precisely what you want;

- Focus and take action, otherwise your desires will always remain mere dreams;

- Start with a target because <u>you can't hit one if you don't have one.</u>

PRACTICE SAFE STRESS
TO MAXIMIZE PROFITS

By

Barry Roberts

Barry Roberts is one of the country's favorite motivation speakers. He is the author of the highly acclaimed book, "PRACTICE SAFE STRESS". His programs are designed to minimize day to day stress by using one's inner sense of humor. Custom designed to meet the specific needs of business groups, civic and social conferences; his engaging delivery informs and delights his audiences while leaving a lasting impact on them.

Roberts says because today's business environment is filled with anxiety, fear, turmoil, and stress that strains and drains our emotional system, causing us to be unable to perform at our highest potential, we need to learn to successfully minimize stress. We must strive to become more efficient, productive, creative and profitable. Practice Safe Stress is an informative publication with cutting edge theories.

The information teaches one to become more productive, regain one's competitive edge; improve relations with clients and co-workers and approach each and every day with a more cheerful attitude.

Roberts insures the reader that PSS is not about telling jokes, but a means to help get through any stressful situation interfering with a quality of life and work.

The author has developed a presentation he calls L.I.F.E. (laughter, introspection, five minute fun flings, enthusiasm/energy). It is fun and fast paced, and allows the attendees to learn simple techniques that will help make every day cheerful, enthusiastic, productive and creative.

During conference breaks, Roberts changes the energy in the room by using Five Minute Fun Flings, such as play yo-yo; visualize someone who is causing you stress looking like a cartoon character; make up a funny caption for photos in newspapers and magazines; and play an 'air-guitar' as you listen to music.

Another set of diversions for break times are: (1) enter a crowded elevator, get out on the next floor, run up and down and very casually, get back on again; (2) read a travel brochure, close your eyes and imagine you're there; and (3) call a friend, tell them you have learned a foreign language. Then read the paper or some article backwards to them. Keep in mind; just concentrate on anything you can do to ignite your sense of humor. It will be time well spent.

Roberts is also a qualified Laugh Instructor who has completed the World Laughter studies and supervised training on the Science of Laughter and Healing with laugh strategies as prescribed by the WLT Code of Ethics.

After one of Barry's presentations, a director said to him, "You started our annual meeting off with a bang! I, like so many members, took notes and will implement them into our daily schedule. We thank you for being a part of our conference and for bringing in the sunshine."

A Blonde's View

"I got fired from my pharmacy job for failing to print labels on bottles. The bottles won't fit in the printer!"

"I got really excited. I finished jigsaw puzzle in 6 months. The box said 2-4 years."

LAUGHTER YOGA CLUBS

Where Laughter has become the Business of Health

"When you laugh, you change. When you change the whole world changes around you."

Ten years ago, Dr. Madan Kataria, a physician, founded the first Laughing Club in India. Dr. Kataria had what he called a flash of inspiration after years of observing how his patients' immune systems improved following bouts of laughter. He developed a new technique of "thought-free" group laughter based on yoga. Dr. Kataria gradually fine-tuned his daily regimen of laughter exercises to a near science and has since formed more than 6,000 clubs in Europe, the Far East, Australia, America and Africa.

Laughter Yoga is a physically oriented technique that uses a perfect blend of playful, empowering and otherwise "tension-releasing" simple laughter exercises, interspersed with gentle breathing and stretching, rhythmic clapping and chanting of ho, ho, ha, ha, ha, ha in unison. the goal of this new revolution is to improve health, increase wellness and promote peace through personal transformation. In Laughter yoga, laughing is used as a tool, not an emotion.

Sebastien Gendry sums up Laughing Yoga as, Non-political, non-religious, non-racial, non-threatening and non-competitive. It comes with no-strings attached. There are no jokes or comedy and no judging. It interrupts the power struggle and breaks down the instinctive barriers between people. On a deeper level, it proves that pain can be overcome and shows that we can all live in peace together. It is now indisputable that laughter plays a role in healing, staying healthy, controlling stress reactions and maintaining emotional balance. Laughter has been rediscovered as a powerful tool in the battle against many mental and physical diseases.

Laughter Yoga teaches emotional resilience: how to make happiness a choice and not a consequence, and how to respond positively, even in the face of adversity. Should you laugh every day? **Only if you want to feel good!**

Steve Wilson, founder of the World Laughter Tour, Inc. has been teaching the therapeutic benefits of laughter since 1984. He brought Dr. Kataria to America for a lecture tour. They visited 14 cities in seven weeks and as a result, launched the World Laughter Tour. Wilson's Columbus-based business has trained 450 laugh leaders and seeded at least 200 laughter clubs.

Wilson speaks of the peace-giving aspects of laughter. He said, "It's a way to avoid intense and difficult emotions. It's part of my spiritual practice, and it is the easiest form of meditation..." Wilson believes that war exists because there is so much war inside of us as individuals. He explains that the power of laughter helps diffuse those hard emotions which bring people together. Wilson is called the world's leading Joyologist.

His passion is to lead the world to health, happiness and peace through laughter.

UNIVERSITY OF LIVING LIFE

Dr. Kataria announced recently that the University of Living Life, the world's first international university of Laughter Yoga will be build in Bangalore City, India. In the first phase, Dr. Kataria said, " We're building a complex of 40 rooms and a community hall for about 500 people. There will be training centers and treatment rooms where students will be taught how to bring good health, joy and laughter into their lives."

The building of Bangalore's ULL is underway. To fulfill the dream of making the world more peaceful, the second university is scheduled for Australia, followed by America, Europe and finally Africa. Students and Certified Laugh Leaders will be recruited from the 65 countries and millions of practitioners for the 20 plus University departments. for information, you may contact Dr. Katara at mk@laughteryoga.org.

Aaaaaah Laughter

"The healthiest response to life is LAUGHTER There is always a reason to be grateful you belong in the scheme of the universe There is nothing to be afraid of. You are safe. Your soul cherishes every aspect of your life. There is a plan, and your soul knows what it is. Ecstasy is the energy of spirit. When life flows, ecstasy is natural. There is a creative solution to every problem. Every possibility holds the promise of abundance. Obstacles are opportunities in disguise. Evolution leads the way through desire. Freedom is letting go."

Deepak Chopra

BLESSINGS

"When such as I cast out remorse
So great a sweetness flows into the breast
We must laugh and we must sing
We are blest by everything
Everything we look upon is blessed?
William Butler Yeates

*"I am the smile on the faces of the flowers and
In each soul, I am the Wisdom and Power that
Sustains all creation."*
Paramhansa Yogananda

PARENTING WITH HUMOR & LAUGHTER

"We never really grow up. We only learn how to act in public."

RX LAUGHTER STUDY

If you are a parent, you know that infants begin smiling during the first weeks of life and laugh out loud within months of being born. At UCLA's Jansson Cancer Center, Psychiatrist Margaret Stuber M.D., a researcher, partnered with the nonprofit organization, RX Laughter, to study use of laughter to help children and adolescents better handle painful procedures. Dr. Stuber spent her days showing kids funny videos. The researchers are trying to figure out whether pediatricians should be prescribing laughter to help heal sick children. "What I am hoping for, is nothing less than revolutionizing the way we treat kids," Stuber said. Ever since Norman Cousins claimed to have laughed himself out of terminal disease, scientists and researchers added Cousins' theory to the test. So far the results have been very promising.

THE FIRST LAUGH RITE

The desire to be with people who laugh or make us laugh must be universal. Renea Arnold, Dr. Struber's colleague, said, "In our office, we are fortunate to have our own resident 'giggle bug'. At 16 months old, our colleague's son laughs at the drop of a hat. It's such fun to hear Kieran laugh that when he comes into the office, we are all competing to see who can make him laugh first."

Parents have always found joy when their babies begin to laugh.

The Navajo Indians place such value on humor that when a child laughs out loud for the first time, the milestone is celebrated and honored with 'The First Laugh Rite'. But where does this laughter come from? In Paul McGhee's Understanding and Promoting the Development of Children's Humor, we're told that, "Children's sense of humor reflects their new intellectual achievements. Humor is basically a form of play; play with ideas."

Further, humor is generally the funniest during the months after the children can first understand a level of jokes. Kids respond to riddles when they reach first and second grade. But become progressively less funny after it becomes too easy for them. So the question becomes, how can we contribute to the development of children's cheerfulness? One of the ways is by choosing books and rhymes for story time that match children's ages and current intellectual abilities.

Babies in the first year most often laugh when their parents are making silly faces or sounds. Hearing rhyming words, like piggly-wiggly, or the fun animal sounds, can make a baby laugh. Most babies enjoy the sensation of their bodies moving through space. In a safe way, like the ups and downs in the nursery rhyme "The Noble Duke of York". Although some bouncing rhymes can be rather startling at first, most babies love the surprise of "falling off" of dad's knee when chanting "Mother and Father and Uncle John."

Before long, babies trust that Dad won't let them fall. Babies, who are feeling uneasy in a situation, may change a furrowed brow to a giggle of relief when they learn there's nothing to fear.

THE CANNON TWINS ARRIVE
Applause...Applause

Internationally renowned singer Mariah Carey and husband Nick Cannon, former Disney Kid and present host of TV's America's Got Talent, celebrated the birth of Twins in June of 2011.

Describing the big moment during an interview on TV's "The Talk", the excited, first time Dad said "I directed the big baby show with the cast of doctors, nurses and family". It really was an incredible gift from God. I had set up the hospital birthing room with video camera, lights and the music tape as I waited for the big moment. Then when the doctor said those famous words "Push mother, push" I turned on the lights, cued the music and the room filled with the sound of Mariah's Madison Square Garden concert with the applause of thousands. What a Welcome! I announced "you have just witnessed the first stage appearance of the Cannon Twins".

A few minutes and lots of kisses and congratulations later you could hear Mariah saying "Nick, turn the lights and the camera off and get my make-up girl in here".

Everyone laughed while I turned off the camera, called the young lady who began the transformation.

The next frames on the tape showed the beautiful new Mommy propped upon the bed, smiling and posing in a gorgeous lace gown, with the twins (boy and girl) on pink and blue satin pillows, surrounded by family and friends As if waiting for the director's final words. Nick in fact did say, "cut, cut that's a wrap. Good show everybody."

Now folks, that's how "Stars Are Born"!!

"I knew I was an unwanted baby when I saw that my bath toys were a toaster and a radio."

Joan Rivers.

THERE WERE NAPS

Comedy writer Gary Rudoren has become a famous role model for parenting. His amazing story about raising his twins, Lev and Shayna with humor has been the delight of thousands.

"I am not one of those parents with a million rules, but there is one thing I insist on: The first thing my kids should see when they wake up from their naps is a smile. For good measure, after naps I usually jump up and down when I walk into their room to show how excited I am to see them.

This is clearly one of those things you can do as a stay at home dad that you cannot do as a stay at work dad in the office. When the twins were babies, I'm fairly certain they thought they were about to be attacked by a crazed giant. Since the age of 18 months or so, they would stand up in their cribs and jump up and down with me as I exclaimed, "Naps are over! Naps are over," like a victory dance in an undeclared war against sleep."

Early on in this rollercoaster ride of raising kids, it struck me that among the many responsibilities of being a parent was my need to make sure that my children learned what's funny. Especially how to BE funny. I'm a comedy writer and I guess, like any Dr. Dad or Dad, Esq., I secretly hoped that my children might want to get into the 'family business'. Even if it turns out that they just have to be a doctor or must be a lawyer, I want them to be the funniest ones they can be. I felt I would help them grow into a wonderfully engaged human being we hoped they would become. Also appreciating comedy seemed like a tangible skill I could teach them myself. Fatherhood gave me a mission. My twins are my little lab experiments, my own young Frankensteins.

I started on this journey with laughing lessons. From the time my son Lev and my daughter, Shayna, were little, maybe three months old, I would place them on our bed after naps. Unable to roll over, they were just where I wanted them.

I'd look down into their tiny little faces and begin chanting, "Ha, ha, ha, ha, ha...Hee, hee, hee, hee, hee...Hi, hi,hi, hi, hi,...Ho, ho, ho, ho, ho,...Huu, huu, huu, huu, huu.

It's not enough to just say this series of rhythmic syllables. You have to believe it. Sell it. I would rub my hands around my Santa-sized stomach and continue the chant. It took a while, but eventually I earned some big smiles. Sometimes even some spit ups.

I added my bits in my routine. I'd rub my tummy, do a bit of a jig, bop my big head around, and mix in a few loud and loving raspberries on their bellies. I have no scientific fact to back this up, but I firmly believe my twins discovered laughing earlier than most because of our daily lessons. Or, maybe it's because the sessions were often conducted in my underwear.

Then we moved on to facial comedy. The bug-eyes. The cross-eyes. The double-takes. Even a little spit-take just to show them that grown-ups do it too, and with the right comic timing, it isn't just disgusting.

After every bit, I'd laugh, to reinforce the lessons and show the munchkins that I was a friendly giant.

On those oh-so-rare days when the twins were a little off their game, and the chanting, and facial comedy weren't working, I'd pull out my absolute killer, can't lose 'Rockettes' bit. this is where I started singing something rockin' like a Springsteen song and put their tiny little legs in my hands and dance them back and forth, building a rhythm I imagine even the 'Boss' would admire. This technique, which I humbly declare to have invented, has proven to be fool proof: I always get the laughs. I walk off the baby-stage confident that I've nailed it.

I admit that I like looking silly and stupid in front of my kids. I only hope that by embracing fatherhood the way I have, and by assuming the heavy responsibility of being their comedy mentor, I have started Lev & Shayna on the road to a more joyful life.

WHY LAUGHTER IS A SIGN OF LEARNING

Emily Perimen Abedon says her one year old son, River, has earned the nickname, "Giddyup Boy", because he giggles heartily at funny faces, howls at peekaboos and awards any silly antics with big time belly laughs. For her husband, Todd, and their four children, they enjoy the moments of pure joy that Giddy-up Boy brings them.

Having a sense of humor plays an important role in developing self-esteem, learning to problem solve and honing social skills. Anyone who's watched Comedy Central can attest that humor takes a wide variety of forms in word play, visual jokes or simply using the element of surprise. Most experts agree that the root of humor is taking something in its familiar form and turning it upside down, makes it offbeat and an attention grabber.

Starting around six months old, "peekaboo" becomes a funny bone favorite and almost anything that is decidedly out of their ordinary realm of experience gives kids the giggles.

One father of five talks about his one year old son Charles, who cracks up when he pretends to drink out of a sippy cup. "As soon as I put it in my mouth, he screams with laughter. I'm his favorite comedian." Understanding that Daddy is a grown-up and doesn't drink out of sippy cups is where a child's sense of humor begins, explains Dr. Paul E. McGhee, A developmental psychologist and author of Understanding a Promoting the Development of Children's Humor.

A child's sense of humor really takes flight when he starts enjoying imaginative play around age three. Showing up in Mom's high heels to get Grandma laughing, changing the ending of a favorite song to nonsense words, or even telling silly knock-knock jokes expresses intellectual growth.

ANOTHER SIDE OF PARENTING

A Stanford University professor revealed an interesting study. He found that all babies below the age of four are near genius level for child intelligence.

But something starts to happen after this age. The child's capabilities start waning. Some continue to show a high intelligence level while others stumble and slow down. The professor believes that children slow down because limitations are drummed into their minds by their parents, teachers and friends as well as movies and other media programming directed to them.

Parents scream, "Don't say such silly things!" "Stop playing with your imaginary friend. He does not exist!" "No, silly, that's wrong. You are so stupid!" The list goes on. When you learn that you can go beyond your forced limitations, you can castaway your fears and pick up skills beyond the ordinary, and also realize you can cast away all these limitations and experience the potential you may have had hiding away in your mind since you were four-years-old.

So, don't say negative things to yourself or your children. You have 'geniuses' to parent.

NINE WAYS TO TEASE A CHILD OUT OF A BAD MOOD

1. Inform him that he needs all that negative stuff drained out and to be filled with happy thoughts instead. Suggest something he's be appalled by like painting pink daises on his toenails.

2. Imitate the whining he's doing and morph it into the whine of a race car. Rev the engine through a few gears, then make the sounds of a car screeching to a halt and crashing.

3. Tickle Fight!

4. Give him pointers on how to make his pouting more effective.

5. Rate his pout on a scale of 1 to 10

6. Throw your own fit. Make it big. Really put your all into it. (Not in public).

7. Pin him down and kiss him all over his face until he starts laughing.

8. Initiate a quick competition, "who can jump the highest?" Any kind of physical competition works as long as you get him up and moving a bit.

9. Always get your child to laugh before his morning goodbye kiss.

"What do you call a monkey in a minefield? A Ba-boom."

Anonymous

USING HUMOR AS A PARENTING TOOL

By Ron Huxley

Humor is a parenting tool that has saved many parents from potentially abusive situations. Humor can act as a release valve for all the stress that accumulates during the day between parents and children. Raising children is a challenge, during the best of times. During the worst of times, it can be extremely frustrating.

Humor can take many forms. One application is for parents, during a stressful situation, to laugh at themselves. We all make mistakes and chuckling at ourselves during these dangerous moments can not only relieve the tension in the room but can also teach your child that life shouldn't be treated so seriously. By laughing at themselves, parents can show their children that one's self-esteem is not based on what you do (a conditional attitude) but on who you are (an unconditional attitude).

Parents can also make a soft joke of their child's mistake. These jokes should be in good taste and take into consideration the sensitivity level of the child. Some children are crushed by what others would consider a harmless jest. Remember, the object of this parenting tool is to decrease stress not increase bad feelings. This second application of humor also teaches children that life shouldn't be treated too seriously. It encourages children to pick themselves up, dust themselves off, and go on after a mistake was made.

An example of a tool in action might include the stressful situation of getting everyone ready for work and school in the morning. If on the way to school, parents sense a dark cloud in the car, they can utilize this parenting tool. Parents can change the mood by singing a funny lyric or telling a knock-knock joke to keep the mood affable. Children will get into the spirit of the humor by telling their own jokes, even if they are made up on the spot.

REV. JAMES FORD...THE STORYTELLER

For the past 25 years, Pastor James E. Ford has entertained, educated and energized thousands of people with his very unique and matchless presentation style. Whether he's preaching, teaching or merely holding a one on one,

Pastor Ford celebrates God's Gift of Laughter. To hear him in a college auditorium, a conference hall, a classroom or mall, on the radio, at his church or on the street corner, you will be mesmerized by the complexity of valued information blended with the joyfulness of his humor. He is truly unforgettable.

A tireless educator, minister and business consultant, Pastor Ford emphasizes the importance of devotion to the work you do, how to discover your inner passion, how to acquire habits of persistence, as well as developing deeper spiritual awareness.

Rev. Ford and wife Michelle are the founders of *Three Plus Me, Inc*. Its focus is the prevention of drug use and violence and a strong concentration on academic excellence.

His organization and church seek to change the thinking of people of all ages and stages, so that their members and audiences can learn to choose how to live a happier, healthier way of life.

Pastor Ford says "*we live in a world of wanderers which means to go about aimlessly without a plan or fixed destination*". He calls this a 'sickness of the focus and a disease of desire.' But he assures us to "take heart, there is a cure and it already lies within you".

Pastor Ford conducts his "Motivation By Inspiration" workshops for his radio audiences, on DVRs, in person and in many publications.

One of his lessons entitled "**How To Have An A+ Child In A D-World**" has become one of his most ordered DVDs. He believes that the overwhelming majority of parents deeply love their children and want the very best for them. He is convinced that the mistakes parents have made are by and large, mistakes of the head and NOT the heart. Some of his recommendations are: If you're not pleased with your child's output, try changing the input...especially from you.

We all want to be happy, some pursue it, and others create it. Guess who is the happiest? To have hope in the future, one must have power in the present. The most important thing a Father can do for his children is <u>Love Their Mother</u>. You are a parent only when you provide for, protect and prepare your child for life. Parents, if you don't listen to your children's problems they won't listen to your solutions. Rules without relationship, lead to rebellion.

Most families do not communicate, they simply take turns talking. As parents, we must remember that failure is an event...not a person.

The most important subject in America is our children, our kids may not be 100% Of the population, but they definitely are 100% of our future.

Pastor Ford has observed that the average six year old boy, until he's in the first grade, only gets $1/6^{th}$ as much of the hugging and kissing as the average little girl.

Interestingly enough, in the first grade, little boys get in six times as much trouble as little girls and are nine times as likely to have a speech impediment. The FBI has stated there is no record of girls going astray that have received true love from their fathers.

"Zig Zigler quotes: "*Your children, more Attention pay, to what you DO than what you say.*"

CHILDREN LIVE WHAT THEY LEARN

If a child lives with criticism, he learns to condemn;

If a child lives with hostility, he learns violence

If a child lives with ridicule, he learns to be shy

If a child lives with shame, he learns to feel guilty

If a child lives with encouragement, he learns confidence

If a child lives with praise, he learns to appreciate

If a child lives with fairness, he learns justice

If a child lives with security, he learns faith

If a child lives with approval, he learns to like himself

If a child lives with acceptance, and friendship, he

learns to love the world.

>   Rev. James E. Ford, The Storyteller.

"I asked God for a bike, but I know God doesn't work that way. So, I stole a bike and asked for forgiveness."

Anonymous

A TEACHER'S SECRET USE OF HUMOR

Miss Quiana Brownlee was a young teacher in what was referred to as a "tough" school district. Yet she was praised for having well behaved students who also earned decent grades.

One morning before the school bell rang, the principal, Mr. Wilson called Miss Brownlee to his office and asked her if she would share her successful teaching methods with him, adding that her children were failing in other classes and had disciplinary problems. His exact question to her was something along the lines of, "What are you doing to the kids? Hypnotizing them?"

After a laugh or two, Miss Brownlee responded that from day one she told the children, "I have no children of my own, so I am going to treat each of them as my own child.

I expect you to become the smartest, nicest and most respectful young men and women in my world of Algebra. If any of you have difficulties, stay after school with me and we'll find a solution."

"Did that work, Miss Brownlee?" the Principal asked. "Not immediately sir, but if any of them disobeyed, I'd put their names up on the blackboard, never explaining the purpose. At the end of the class, as the children were leaving, every "good" child received a piece of candy and a pat on the back. Those whose names were on the board, I merely said, 'Sorry my Dear, perhaps next time.' It took approximately four weeks, but now I have 100 percent participation. And the best part is their algebra improved.

"We laugh a lot. I have them clap for each other's accomplishments and this led to a break time of 10 minutes, providing all of their work is completed. Our break time is spent telling funny jokes and stories.

I am enjoying teaching more than ever and 'my babies' are doing very well."

Miss Brownlee went on to explain that laughter is healing and it provides positive energy for everyone in the room.

This had been her family's teaching method for over 50 years. She has three sisters and they were able to strengthen the bonds of friendship with not only their students, but with parents as well; all because of the power of humor.

"Well Miss Brownlee, you have taught me a lot in our little talk. I am grateful and I shall spread this joyful concept among our teaching and administrative staff. It may help me weed out some of the teachers who really do not care for personal contact with children. Everyone was not born to teach. It's evident you were. Thanks again. Now, I understand why the district superintendent is considering you for an assistant principal slot.

I hope our school will be lucky enough to get you," said Dr. Wilborn.

"Oh, Dr. Wilborn." replied Miss Brownlee. "I love being in the classroom. I do not want an administrator's post. I was indeed born to teach."

The following year, the district superintendent placed Miss Brownlee at the King's Elementary School as assistant principal with one additional job. At her request she was allowed to continue teaching Algebra until she found a new young teacher who was born to teach and understood how to use 'the teacher's secret'. After her first year, the young Mrs. Osborn won Teacher of the Year. Three years later, Assistant Principal Brownlee was announced as the new principal of King Elementary School during the retirement party for Dr. Wilborn.

> "Life is the most spectacular show on earth. Become one of its brightest stars."
>
> Anonymous

WHAT THE DOCTORS SAY

When you reach a point where your belief in yourself is so strong that you know you can accomplish anything you can put your mind to, your future will be unlimited.

                                          Anonymous

SPEAK IT AS IF

From: *Speaking the Lost Language of God*
        by Gregg Braden

Dr. Braden and fellow scientists at the HeartMath Institute concluded that human emotion is the language that speaks directly to the place where we have access to the healing of our bodies and peace of our world. When we can feel the feelings that we would like to experience in this world, as if they already exists, we literally speak the language to the fundamental life force that can breathe them into existence in our world, body and affairs.

Braden says that prayer is most commonly practiced in the west and has four modalities. Colloquial, Ritualistic, Petitionary and Meditative. Dr. Braden says there is also a fifth. The lost modality of prayer which ancients believe is where you fully experience that which you desire. In this method, the FEELING is the prayer. This type of prayer shows that because we are part of nature we have the language, a nonverbal language, of coherent emotion, to change the events of our life and the world around us. Since we always feel something, we are engaged in a modality of prayer every moment of our lives.

THE POWER OF FEELING

Dr. Braden tells the story about a woman's tumor being 'dissolved' in a medicine-less hospital in China. Three practitioners felt the feeling in their bodies as if the woman's body was already fully healed. By feeling this, they bought the lift force into their bodies knowing that her body would mirror theirs.

They said a mantra which reinforced the feeling that the woman was already healed. The tumor disappeared in three minutes. This hospital had a 90 percent success rate using this kind of technique.

Braden asserts that, "If energy and matter are interchangeable, then feeling and experiences are interchangeable. We must be able to feel that something will happen in our lives, to bring the energy of it into being".

POWER VS. FORCE

In his groundbreaking book Power vs. Force, Sir David R. Hawkins, M.D., Ph.D. often refers to the wonders of laughter, humor, spiritually, physically and emotionally. Dr. Hawkins personally has a tremendous sense of humor which shines through all of his talks. And he believes humor is a vital aspect of the spiritual path.

Dr. Hawkins analyzes the basic nature of human thought and consciousness itself and makes available the key to penetrating the last barrier to the advancement of civilization and science. He details how people may resolve for themselves the most crucial of all human dilemmas...how to instantly determine the truth of falsehood of any statement or supposed fact. He is famous for his I Can Do It conferences held on cruises. He often reminds his students that, "It is not the ego itself that is the problem, but the juice, power or excitement we get out of its pitfalls."

THE POWER OF PLAY

Another internationally acclaimed oncologist, author and speaker is Dr. O. Carl Simonton of the Simonton Cancer Center in California. He is best known for his pioneering insights and research in the field of psychosocial oncology where he developed a model of emotional support for the treatment of cancer patients. An approach that introduced the concept that one's state of mind could influence their ability to survive cancer.

His research established the foundation for two widely acclaimed books which he coauthored, Getting Well Again and The Healing Journey.

At the Simonton Center, Dr. Simonton and staff use the power of play as a mandatory class of activity. Patients revisit their happy days of youth, spending pleasurable hours of laughter and happiness. In recent years, his model has received great acceptance in Germany, Poland, Japan and Switzerland where he routinely conducts training sessions for health professionals. Along with the healing aspects of laughter, games and music, Dr. Simonton continues his quest to help individuals build upon their strengths by enabling them to travel their healing journeys with hope, humor and inspiration.

"A stockbroker urged me to buy a stock that would triple its value every year. I told him, at my age, I don't even buy green bananas."

Claude Pepper

MEDICAL TERMINOLOGY (IN THE SOUTH)

Southerners have the lowest stress rate in America because they do not take medical terminology seriously.

Artery	Study of paintings
Bacteria	Back door to cafeteria
Barium	What doctors do when patients die
Benign	What you be, after you be eight
Cat Scan	Searching for kitty
Cauterize	Made eye contact with her
Dilate	To live late
Fibula	A small lie
Fester	Quicker than someone else
Labor Pain	Getting hurt at work

THE DOCTOR OF WIT AND WISDOM

Oprah Winfrey, the world's greatest teacher, closed her classroom after 25 unparalled years of enlightenment and the unexpected.

Professor O has become life's 'taste-tester'. She finds the opportunities, identifies, defines and redefines that part of life she wants to share with everyone. It's like a mother of a newly hatched bird. She searches for the worms, examines them, chews and finally regurgitates the food for her babies.

> *We are blessed. We have been loaned one of God's Guardian Angels.*
>
> *Anonymous*

Recently, between 'feedings', she wrote in her journal, Oprah on Oprah. What I know for Sure, is that: "One of my greatest lessons has been to fully understand that what looks like a dark patch in the quest for success, is the universe pointing you in a new direction.

Anything can become a miracle, a godsend, an opportunity...if you choose to see it that way. When you see obstacles for what they are, you never lose faith in the path it takes to get you where you want to go. Who you're meant to be, evolves from where you are right now. So, learning to appreciate our best lessons, mistakes, and setbacks as stepping stones to the future, is a clear sign you're moving in the right direction.

To study and prepare for your next degree at the 'Oprah Winfrey University', join Professor O and friends in Life Class. At the beginning of the first semester for more than one million students, Oprah said, "We are both the student and the teacher for each other. The Master Class is the course. Your life is the class room."

BACKSTAGE AT HARPO STUDIOS

One of the Oprah's Show nearly next to 'kin', is Executive Producer and President at Harpo, Sheri Salata who shared these memories. "After joining Oprah in her vegan experiment, I know for sure that water with a little lemon is quite nice. " Three more things Sheri knows are:

Never forget what it's like to be at the bottom. I started at Harpo as a very junior producer. A few months in, Oprah saw something I'd written for a commercial and said, "who wrote this? It's really good." She thanked me for my work and said, "I like your shoes." I lived on that moment for two years.

The best cure for exhaustion is laughter; at the end of a long day of taping two shows, Oprah and I usually had no brainpower left and that's when Oprah would start doing impressions of our fellow staff members, or her spot-on version of Chris Rock. It cracked us up and got us ready to do it all again the following morning.

All will be well. That's my mantra and it's so freeing when you're facing a crisis. When I began this job, every failed booking or on-air slip up felt like a disaster. But after a while I noticed that Oprah wasn't bothered in the least. She's always open to the next good thing that's on its way.

OPRAH WINFREY: EVERYBODY GETS A CAR!

Let me tell you a wonderful story about Oprah's biggest giveaway.

Once upon a time, while walking down West Washington in Chicago, Illinois, I heard a strange, muffled, unidentifiable noise. I smiled, kept walking, a little slower however, until the sidewalk seemed to shake, and I begin to think 'earthquake'. Suddenly all hell (excuse me) pandemonium broke out as I saw The Harpo Studio building and realized that something VERY BIG, was going on at the Oprah Winfrey Show. I stopped, entered the building to this thunderous sound of pure, unadultered, stroke-provoking Joy...powerful enough to send a rocket to the moon by 276 visitors who were squealing, screaming, shrieking, laughing, crying and praying... This was the ULTIMATE response to a Once In A Lifetime Fantasy.

Imagine, if you can, being a guest of the Oprah Winfrey Show and suddenly you hear Oprah say:

(The following is the "You Get A Car" transcript in its entirety) "Cue the drumroll. All right. Open your boxes. Open your boxes!! One-Two-Three! YOU GET A CAR...YOU GET A CAR...YOU GET A CAR EVERYBODY GETS A CAR!

Everybody gets a car! Everybody gets a car! Everybody gets a car! Oh My Goodness!!! Everybody gets a car! You get a car...You get a car! You get a car! WHOA! WHOA!

Is that the wildest? Is that the wildest? Okay. And guess what??? Hold on, hold on, hold on, hold on, HOLD ON...everybody... YOUR CARS ARE WAITING RIGHT OUTSIDE!!!!! The cars are waiting RIGHT OUTSIDE!!!

Whoa, Oh, My God, Oh my God, Whoa...Whoa, Oh My God...THERE THEY ARE....276 BRAND NEW PONTIACS. In the Parking Lots."

****

Winfrey said she chose her audience members based on testimonials from Their friends and family about their specific needs for a new car.

One couple drove a car with more than 400,000 miles on it; another woman drove a car that her son said 'looks like she got into a gun fight."

No doubt about it...Oprah is Phenomenal.

During the Motion Picture Academy event of 2011, where Miss Winfrey was being honored, Quincy Jones and John Travolta said "Miss Winfrey was the most wonderful person in the world, the most magical person in the world, and the most powerful person in the world. Oprah defies easy description. Her indefinable genius has given us faith and hope for the future."

DEFINING HUMOR

A wide variety of disciplines have attempted to define and describe humor. Seemingly, anyone with an opinion has tried to explain what tickles us and makes us laugh.

The word "humor" derives from two words; the Latin word *umor* and the medieval word humor mean fluid. Both were originally medical terms that referred to a biological temperament. According to Webster's dictionary, humor is the quality that makes something seem funny, amusing or ludicrous. Vera Robinson, a nurse who wrote about the use of humor in healthcare setting, defined it as, "Any communication which is perceived by any of the interacting parties as humorous and leads to laughing, smiling and feelings of amusement."

Humor takes you to a higher place where you can view the world from a more relaxed, positive, creative, joyful and balanced perspective. In other words, humor is the interpretation of what you perceive as funny.

Your sense of humor begins forming during your early life lessons of what is appropriate to laugh about or inappropriate (such as ridicule or teasing). Once the perception is processed in our mind, then your mind informs your body to push the laughter button and let your laughter sounds begin.

Dr. Paul McGhee suggests that some people need to surround themselves with humor through comedy clubs, television shows or friends who are identified as having a "great sense of humor". By doing so, Dr. McGhee contends that people will connect with humor and then enjoy the laughter that follows.

Humor is definitely a major form of communication. It relates to delivery of a message and a person's perception of that message. This message may then be interpreted in as many different ways as there are recipients. This leads to humor's subjectivity -- what one person finds funny, another could find offensive. Some people may not even "get it" at all.

Despite such a variety of definitions, the medical community still arrives at the same conclusion: A sense of humor is good for you, both physically and psychologically. Not only does levity provide people with better perspectives on problems, but it frequently offers much-needed relief from worrisome situations that would otherwise add to a person's stress and anxiety.

HUMOR HELPS PROFESSIONALS

For decades, researchers have explored how humor helps patients relieve stress and heal. Melissa B. Wanzer, Ed.D, and professor of Communication studies at Canisius College in Buffalo, N.Y. has taken it one step further with her research on how humor helps medical professionals cope with their difficult jobs. She also looked at how humor affects the elderly and how it can increase communication in the workplace and in the classroom.

Wanzer wondered how health care providers care for terminally ill people and manage to come back to work each day.

So she asked them in large scale studies. Their answer? HUMOR. She found humor to be beneficial in other areas as well.

"If employees view their managers as humor-oriented, they also view them as more effective. Employees also reported higher job satisfaction when they worked for someone who was more humor oriented and used humor effectively and appropriately. Wanzer and her colleagues found that humor is an effective way to cope with on the job stress, again, when used appropriately.

Wanzer teaches a course in "Constructive Uses of Humor" which always fills to capacity. Students are equipped to prepare and perform a stand-up routine in front of the class. But the class is not all fun and games. Students read though journal articles and interpret factual studies on humor. One such case involves Southwest Airlines strategic effort to integrate humor into the workplace, in order to create a positive environment for employees and customers. Her research shows that students report learning more from teachers who use humor effectively."

Humor gives us a different perspective on the many challenges of our complicated lives. If we can make light of the situations, they will no longer be a threat to us.

We have the power to discount its affect. With such an attitude of detachment, we feel a sense of self-protection and control in our environment. Bill Cosby is fond of saying, "If you can laugh at it, you can survive it."

Endogenous opioids are released when we laugh. They bind to the central nervous system naturally produce some of the pharmacological properties of powerful drugs like morphine, with out the dangerous side effects of plant-produced opiates. Opioids are released when we are happy, have an orgasm (especially in a supportive romantic relationship) or exercise vigorously (i.e. *"the runners high"* or *"the dancer's high"*.)

Opioids are addictive. We are highly motivated to return to the happy mental images that make us feel good. Happy humor helps us live longer, healthier, more productive lives.

People with a good sense of humor are much more fun to be around. Have you ever seen a personal ad looking for a partner with NO sense of humor? A merry heart not only is a healthy heart, but it also can lead to many other long-term lifestyle improvements.

Dolphins are so smart that within a few weeks of captivity, they can train people to stand on the very edge of the pool and throw them fish.

Unknown

BECOME A STUDENT COMIC

Taking an improvisational comedy class can be very therapeutic. You will laugh a lot and enjoy the study of endless mechanisms of spontaneous ad hoc humor. Students in a beginning improv comedy class are generous with their laughter which encourages you to experiment with developing your own sense of humor in a friendly social setting. The confidence that comes from knowing that you have a good sense of humor can help lonely depressed people overcome the stress associated with an unhealthy fear of poor social interaction skills.

These classes teach students to listen closely to what others are saying and to enthusiastically live in the moment. These are skills that have many other applications and benefits throughout life. You are never too old to take an improv class. It will greatly enhance your life.

Smiling, holding hands, laughing and dancing can be very happy, healthy activities. Group dance classes can help many people overcome the problem of two left feet. Comedy classes can help improve anyone's understanding of what is and is not funny. Our sense of humor and ability to dance are NOT genetic traits. They are learned intellectually and physical habits and behaviors. The more we understand them, the more we do them, the healthier we will become.

We cannot view humor therapy or any other lifestyle behavior in scientific clinical isolation without also considering the complex mystic/holistic spirit/mind/body benefits that humor has on our entire being, longevity, health, happiness and overall well-being. *A merry heart doeth good like medicine.*

Markus De Lone said, "Humor and most notably laughter, frees the mind, eases the faculties and causes the soul to lift it. Thus, they must not only be looked on as great pleasures but also a superior in the composition of human life."

Evening news is where they begin with, "Good evening," and then proceed to tell you why it isn't.

Unknown

LAUGH 101

Are people born with a sense of humor or is it something one can learn?

Community colleges all over the country are offering free, non-credit courses to help develop or sharpen the 'happy side' of student personalities.

In keeping with the title of this book, one Illinois College is offering a two-part class taught by stand-up comics and humor therapists aimed at improving day to day life through laughter.

The title of the class is "From Humor to Health: Comedy and Healthy Living."

The class does not promise to turn students into professional stand-up comedians, but to show the way to communicate with people can definitely be improved.

Research in this book has already provided the healthy benefits or humor. Dobie Maxwell, a stand-up comic who has taught at Zanies, at Harpers College and a community class in Wisconsin. He said, "We make laughter more a part of student's life style. It's like knowing the secret to walking on water because you know where the rocks are." Check with your community colleges and become a 'stand out' in your circle of friends and family.

THE ESSENCE OF COMEDY

Jerry Seinfeld and Colin Quinn

In the magazine, Curtain Call, Mary Houlihan, a New York Clinical Psychologist, interview friends and fellow stand-up comedians, Jerry Seinfield and Colin Quinn during the Chicago stage production, "Long Story Short". Quinn said, "I'm fascinated by the fact that technology keeps advancing but human nature is exactly the same. He said, "I believe there was probably a Snooki back there somewhere in history."

Seinfeld, one of TV's highest paid comedians, said, "The essence of comedy is all about what you see and how deeply you see beneath the surface of human behavior. That's where humor comes from." To sum up Houlihan's remarks on the life and experiences of the comic. "All comedians who, no matter how much success they have elsewhere, have never given up stand-up. Anyone who goes into stand-up, whether they are successful or not, is immediately addicted to it. They are doing what they love and that cannot be ignored."

Seinfeld likes the freedom of stand-up and feels it's the purest connection of thought to audiences that exists anywhere. Nobody has this connection to a public sensibility as a comedian. He said, "You say it. They hear it. They respond immediately, or they don't. It's a complete hardwire. And that's an intense drug."

In comparing a comic stand-up act with that of TV sitcom, or stage and screen, Quinn Colin said, "In stand-up you can be done with one subject and move on the next. That's part of the charm of stand-up. But, with a show, you have got to stay focused and not play around with things. It's like the difference between short stories and a novel."

HANGIN WITH MR. COOPER

Mark Curry, another memorable stand-up comedian best known for his role as an assistant school teacher on the long running sitcom, "Hangin' with Mr. Cooper." Featured in a documentary recently, he recalled his younger years when comedy saved him from the bad guys in the neighborhood.

He said he found it necessary to walk a certain way, put on a fearless face, confront the gangs with comedic gibberish asking unanswerable funny questions and turn certain danger into a joke It worked. He found that it kept him out of many uncomfortable situations.

CHRISTIAN FUNNY MEN & WOMEN

(Comedian Spank E)

"For years, there has been a growing disconnect between the sensibilities of a large segment of the U.S. and the majority of films and television we see today." So says Mitchell Galin, the executive producer of the first full-length Christian comedy feature ever produced. In the past, Christian comedians have often been stereotyped by critics as being mediocre. That label has been fading over the past years because of a fresh group of rising stars. Creators assure that these comics have a strong history, and that listeners will be rolling in the aisles while at the same time having an enlightening experience. Galin said,

"These comedians express their faith by making people laugh. While apostles of comedy may be imbued with faith and inspiration, it never loses its edge, which makes it relevant to today's audiences."

Comedian Spank E. keeps it clean. Most of us rid ourselves of stress with an occasional dose of comic relief. The after effects one is expecting is usually a renewed and more lighthearted you. Spank E is a gospel comedian who delivers a pleasurable humorous experience that swoons you in the same way but minus the swear words and guild ridden stories. The 18-year industry veteran's stand-up routine has been displayed on BET Comic View and the nationwide Funny Bone Comedy Club chain. His act is absorbed with purpose, while his anointed ambition radiates throughout.

Spank E told N'Digo's, Juel Grange about the drawbacks of keeping it clean and using God-given talent to amuse the soul. As a protégé of the late Bernie Mac. Spank E. learned the business and entertainment side of show business.

Bernie taught him that show business is 90 percent business and 10 percent show as well as how to do contracts and negotiate. He learned timing -- how to be confident in his material and how to create his persona on stage and how to know who Spank E is. Bernie said, "Be yourself, don't change. That's another reason I decided to go into gospel comedy.

Using God's gift for the purpose he intended it be used. That's really where I feel comfortable.

Grange asked Spank E to recall any backlash or criticism that he received from his keep it clean act. He said, I did a clean show in a club recently that was not very well received at first. They were going with it until they found out and said, "Hey wait a minute he's not cursing." Then when they realized they could actually accept a clean show, they came around. It was a shock though. The only other backlash is that I was up there delivering clean comedy and they really wanted to hear the Def Comedy Jam style of humor.

He also revealed that he is fluent in American Sign Language (ASL) and incorporates in his act. He still performs in front of a deaf and hard of hearing audiences from time to time.

Spank E. will be appearing in a new feature film in the called, "Losers Take All".

He also has developed a national gospel comedy tour, along with Lady Luncha Bell from Chicago and four gospel comedians called, "Thou Shall Laugh" which the USO is taking overseas to perform for troops.

Spank E. said, "This is what I meant by using God's gift for the purpose he intended it to be used. It's about the ministry; the comedy is just the vehicle being used to deliver the message."

THE CLOWN PRINCE OF PHYSICIANS

Dr. Hunter "Patch" Adams, Founder of the Gesundheit! Institute, (German for good health) was built outside of Hillsboro in Pocahontas County, West Virginia in 1971. It is staffed by a great group of healers, visionaries and doctors who have integrated a traditional hospital with alternative medicine, such as naturopathy, acupuncture and homeopathy. Their generous and compassionate care also includes performing arts, crafts, nature, agriculture and recreation. One of the institute's missions involves the concept of "humanitarian clowning". The project uses the theme of laughter as an element of effective doctoral care. Years ago, the Institute took clowns into the war zones In Bosnia, refugee camps in the Republic of Macedonia as well as South African orphanages.

As a young physician in Washington, DC, Patch Adams, an in-credible doctor of wit and passion, became so seriously involved in his work that he became deeply depressed.

Foregoing an attempted suicide, Patch committed himself to a mental facility, where he had a revelation which led to the discovery of healing power of humor and love.

Taking classes at a clown school, he learned how to combine humor and clowning into his medical practice. Patch soon realized that patients, who were full of religious faith and had a sense of humor, needed less medication. His belief was "*if you have a strong value system that enriches your life, then your health is going to be affected*".

Because of Dr. Adam's success, many doctors followed his example. In 1998, the movie PATCH ADAMS starring Robin Williams became a blockbuster film that captured the concept of humor as a healing power.

GODS VS. MAN

A group of scientists were sitting around discussing which one would go to God and tell Him that they didn't need Him anymore. One of the scientists volunteered and went off to deliver him their decision. The scientist said, "God we have been thinking that we really don't need you anymore. We've been coming up with great theories and ideas. You know we've cloned sheep and are on the verge of cloning humans. So, you can take a break for a while. No hard feelings okay? But before I go, why don't we have a contest." God said okay. What kind of contest do you have in mind? The scientist said, "A man-making contest." God agreed. The scientist bends down and picks up a handful of dirt and says, "Okay, I'm ready." God replies, "No, no, no. You go and get your own dirt."

PRESENTING LORETTA LAROCHE –

Modern Application of Humor Therapy

Loretta LaRoche is an exciting comedian with a wellness agenda. She is often featured on PBS and serves on the faculty of Boston's Mind-Body Institute. In her hilarious presentations, Loretta dispenses practical wisdom laced with frequent belly laughs while she lampoons the human potential movement and subtly delivers its most important messages. She demonstrates that laughter is important for reducing stress and maintaining a healthy life. Her comedy routines encourage audiences to look for the humor in every situation and use it to defuse stress.

LaRoche suggests using the power of humor to overcome the stress that is in all of our lives. Personal stories, told with heavy New York/Italian sarcasm, show that life is too short to sweat the small stuff. She believes in food and fun to smooth the bumps on the road of life. A recipe for her grandmother's spaghetti sauce is a riotous inclusion.

Her live presentation style is at a steady fast rate that sounds like spontaneous improvisation, but it is based on decades of outstanding work in professional stress management. Her voice, body language and facial expressions have natural ups and downs that create funny expressions and a believable conversational style.

LaRoche says, "I'm always reminding people that the one constant you can count on is that things happen and usually when you're not in the mood for them." She says, "Buy something silly and wear it. A Groucho Marx nose, mustache and glasses are my favorite. When the stress seems unbearable, when you've really reached the limits of your endurance, go into the bathroom, look into the mirror, put on your glasses and ask yourself, 'How serious is this?"

"One night I greeted my husband, Bob, at the door wearing nothing but his wing-tipped shoes. I was laughing hysterically about how I looked. Bob didn't crack a smile. Instead, he bellowed, "What are the neighbors going to think"? I replied, "I don't know. I haven't shown them, yet."

"Most of us don't realize what an impact we have on the world around us. A positive energy field is going to affect others in a beneficial way, even if you don't notice it at first. Why not ask for a standing ovation once in a while? When you go into the office, announce, "I came in. It wasn't easy. I could have gone somewhere else. I'd like a standing ovation if you please."

Light travels faster than sound. This is why some people appear bright until you hear them speak.

Unknown

A HOLY HUMOR HISTORY OF 'AN ECUMENICAL MIRACLE'

During my delightful research for LAUGH AGAIN, I ran across a celebratory issue covering the history of The Joyful Noiseletter (JN). What a joy indeed. Commemorating its 25th anniversary, the newsletter speaks to a nation within a nation of happy Christians, their churches, pastors and congregations.

They spread their joy to like-minded people of all faiths, including Jewish, Moslems, Buddhists and Hindu friends and a large secular humanists group of subscribers. Cal and Rose Samra are the faithful, spirited creators and publishers of this phenomenal publication. They constantly thank God for bringing people together in good humor, civility, and camaraderie, qualities missing in our modern world.

As they described the blessed beginning of JN, I learned about the hundreds of talented volunteer staff of writers, editors, cartoonists who came on board because they believed that they could all learn from one another and that they had much more in common than they had differences.

ITS DIVINE COMEDY

After 25 years of phenomenal growth with hundreds of thousands of subscribers and readers, Dan Runyon of Christianity Today says, "This nondenominational ministry measures its success not by counting dollars, but by watching people laugh.

The Joyful Noiseletter's Board of 40 consulting editors includes not only respected Christian leaders but also an array of denominational representations. The Joyful Noiseletter prints humor that is tasteful and reverent."

The multi-talented comedian Steve Allen, an eloquent advocate for clean comedy since his days as the host of NBCTV's "Tonight Show", said, "We live in a culture bombarded morning, noon and night with messages from films, TV, print media, radio and recordings. It is almost impossible to escape encouragement to act in ways that have traditionally been the province of the libertine, thuggish, coarse, and depraved. Many popular comedians are horrified at what has happened to the beautiful and socially necessary act of comedy. The element of humor is necessary to human beings, necessary for the maintenance of sanity."

The history issue of the JN was so informative. Rose who is also a healer, shared much about the joy found in the Christian Bible.

She said the old and new testaments have 287 references to joy, gladness, merriment, rejoicing, delighting and laughing. She said she was surprised to discover that on the very eve of Jesus' crucifixion, he admonished his disciples at the Last Supper by saying, "These things I have spoken to you, that my joy may be in you and your joy may be full. (John 15:11). Rose commented, "Joy! here is a man about to be arrested, tried, cursed, beaten, spit upon, humiliated, tortured, crucified and He's talking about Joy!"

Cartoonist Bill Keane observed in one of JN's issues that "My friends Erma Bombeck and Art Buchwalk have done far more for health of humanity than Madame Curie or Dr. Christian Barnard."

One of JN's medical consulting editors, Dr. Donald L. Cooper, a Presbyterian, is a nationally recognized authority on sports medicine and physical fitness. He was appointed by President Ronald Reagan to the President's Council on Physical Fitness and Sports.

He was also the football team physician at Oklahoma State University in Stillwater, OK. His wit and humor made him in much demand as a speaker. Dr. Cooper had these suggestions for persons suffering from depression: (1) Keep talking to doctors, counselors, pastors and friends. (2) Never medicate yourself. Let the professionals prescribe the medication. (3) Cultivate a sense of humor and (4) Hang on to your family.

A friend of Dr. Cooper, Dr. Rex Russell, authored an outstanding book titled, What the Bible Says about Healthy Living." It advises using good nutrition, regular exercise and Biblical wisdom to improve your health and lift your spirits. He recommended many of the foods which the folks in the old and new testaments ate.

JN writes, "Jesus was no gloomy Messiah. We know that children were attracted to Jesus and flocked to be near him. In any age, children are never comfortable with melancholy, stern, grumpy people. It was clear that Jesus was the antidepressant of the early Christians. Jesus, the 'Great Physician', was also a very physical Messiah.

A carpenter by trade, he walked great distances every day in a hilly countryside and climbed mountains. He ate a natural Mediterranean diet and clearly was very physically fit."

Here is another delightful celebration I learned from the Joyful Noiseletter. Rev. Dr. Karl R. Kraft of Glassboro, N.J. designed the fun filled Holy Humor Sunday Services, the annual celebration of Jesus' resurrection on the Sunday after Easter. Its popularity has become a happy widespread event.

THE SMILING CHRIST

One of the greatest contributions JN received was the painting of "The Risen Christ by the Sea" by Jack Jewell. Jack was an elderly artist living in a small Massachusetts seaport. His friend, Rev. Martin Clarke, a JN subscriber, was one of the chaplains to the New York Fire Department. Clark asked Jewell to paint a representation of a joyful, smiling Risen Christ. Rev. Clark was the predecessor to the chaplain Rev. Mychal Judge who was killed Sept. 11, 2001 in the attacks on the World Trade Center.

At the urging of Rev. Clarke, Jack Jewell painted and donated the painting to Cal and Rose and it became JN's logo in 1990. The painting has since enjoyed phenomenal grass roots popularity, appearing in church sanctuaries, social halls, conference and retreat centers, religious schools and hospitals all over the country. Many see it as a representation of "The Easter Laugh", God's last laugh on the devil. When he raised Jesus from the dead. On the back of the large print are these scripture verses:

"These things I have spoken to you, that my joy may be in you, and that your joy may be full." (John 15:11)

"When you fast, do not put on a gloomy look as the hypocrites do." (Matt 6:16)

"Happy are you who weep now; you shall laugh." (Luke 6:21)

"Be of good cheer, I have overcome the world." (John 16:33)

"The One whose throne is in Heaven sits laughing." (Psalm 2:4)

This glorious publication is truly a gift to many hundreds of thousands of people who have been touched by this monthly newsletter including me. Operating on a very small budget, JN began in the basement of Cal and Rose's home and is still making 'a joyful noise to the Lord' in the same basement office. We wish them God's continuous blessings of health, joy, and growth.

> *"What a treasury of ho-ho holy humor. Let us bow our head and laugh."*
>
> *The Holy Noiseletter.*

THE LAST GOLDEN GIRL STANDING

BETTY WHITE

"Some people cause happiness wherever they go. Others whenever they go."

Unknown

Betty White, American's sweetheart, is one of the hottest comedians in the country today. Her popularity hit a new peak and the nation's love affair with Betty seems to grow stronger with each passing year. White has been called a National Treasure. She loves playing up her public image as a flirtatious senior citizen.

Betty is the author of the book, If You Ask Me: (And of Course You Won't). Robert Pattinson, known for his role as a vampire, was quoted on White's book jacket, although the lady herself says she doesn't know much about the vampire. She's happy for the compliments he extended but I think he needs to go see a therapist, she joked.

Twenty five years ago, talk show legend Johnny Carson described Betty as, "Somewhere between Mother Theresa and a Call Girl." In one of her TV roles, she gave one of her left-handed compliments to another actress by sweetly saying, "I wish I could wear old clothes as well as you do."

Another show where she was interacting with Mary Tyler Moore who excitedly announced, "I am having Prince William on my show next week." Betty naively responded, "Oh how wonderful Mary, you two would make a marvelous couple. But then, you are too old, American and common." In a monologue, on Saturday Night Live, Betty was describing what it's like being 90 years old. she wrung her hands and sadly said, "Well, if I wanted to connect with my old friends, I'd need a Ouji Board."

Ace Frehlay, former guitarist for Kiss and Tell, an author of the book, No Regrets...Rock n Roll Memoir, loves Betty White so much he uses her name as a code name to decide whether or not to attend a party, i.e., phone rings. Caller asks Ace to come to a party. Ace replies, "Is Betty going to be there?"

Betty has spent seven decades in show business. She was named, The Most Trusted Celebrity in show business. Her response was, "Oh do I have them fooled."

She appeared on the Brian Williams show, "Rock Center" during the holiday and Brian asked Betty what she thought about Regis who just turned 80, retiring. She said, "I tried to talk him out of leaving, but he said no. I'm through. I wonder what in the world he's going to do now. He's so young."

Brian told Betty that he has always remembered and loved that census taker skit she did with Tina Fey.

Sketch: *Tina Fey rings the doorbell and Betty White answers.*

Tina: Good morning Mrs. I am the census taker. What is your name?

Betty: My name is Hilda Flooszenflaba.

Tina: Would you mind spelling that for me?

Betty: Certainly. S M I T H.

One of Betty's recent books is, Betty & Friends: My Life at the Zoo." White still does stand-up. She rips off a joke or two whenever she has a stage. The Hollywood Legend made a joke about dating Charlie Chaplin while accepting the BAFTA Los Angeles Britannic Award for Excellence in Comedy. As Betty lifted her statue, a likeness of Chaplin, she chuckled, "No matter what you may have heard, Chuck Chaplin and I never had a relationship. Well, maybe once."

Betty was quoted at another event saying, "Once a cobra bit my leg. After five days of excruciating pain, the cobra died."

COMEDIANS: SINBAD & STEVE HARVEY

While on tour in Chicago, Sinbad talked to Adeshine Emanual of the Sun Times, about his career, sense of humor and harsh Hollywood lessons. The very popular stand-up comic said, "One way to realize you're doing okay is when people come up to you and say, "Oh I thought you were dead."

Sinbad described how he was enjoying this new tour. "It's just family," he says. He refers to it as more a hybrid reality sitcom than a reality show. Among the many appearances on TV, HBO specials and movies, he said that he has been learning the importance of staying independent. "I always knew from day one they weren't going to understand what I was trying to do, but I didn't care. When you have a point of view and you say I'm not doing that, I have another way of doing that to make it 'smart'. They have issues with that. I should have never looked to Hollywood for anything. And that's what I'm doing in 2012. I'm going back to what I really am. If you get me, you get me. If you don't, get off the track. The train is coming through."

ACT LIKE A WOMAN/THINK LIKE A MAN

Those words put the name Steve Harvey on the international stage. His first book by that title sold 2 million copies to date and opened in theaters as a movie in April 2012.

Steve is a stand-up comic, host of his own radio show, author of several best-selling books, host of TV's Family Feud and now wears the title of Relationship Expert. As such, he is becoming one of talk shows favorite guests (how does he cover all these bases?).

From the stage of The Anderson Cooper Show, Steve gave the following advice, "Female fans complain about men as creatures who won't change." He went on to say, "Man is willing to change, ladies, but it will be for that 'Special Woman'. When she comes along, it's a done deal."

Another bit of advice Steve gave was that there should be a probation period of at least 90 days before a woman 'awards' her new male friend with her 'cookies'.

> *"A celebrity is a person who works hard all his life to become well known, then wears dark glasses to avoid being recognized."*
>
> Red Allen

THE WORLD STILL LOVES LUCY

"God wanted the world to laugh and He invented you, Lucy. Many are called, but you were chosen."

Sammy Davis Jr. speaking to Lucille Ball at the 1984 tribute in her honor.

Thanks to Lucy's determination and physical comedy prowess, she was always ready to take a pie in the face, stomp on a tub full of grapes, or stuff chocolates into her mouth until her face resembled a puffer fish to make unforgettable episodes that are still popular today. Along with her husband, Desi Arnez and friends Vivian Vance as Ethel and William Frawley as Fred, the I Love Lucy series are still the world's most watch comedy shows.

Two TV stations joined the century celebration by running Lucy all day marathons during August 2011. At the Jamestown, N.Y. play house fans watched the series on vintage 1950 television sets.

Susan Ewing, director of group sales at the Lucille Ball-Desi Arnez Center says the Center's mission is to not only preserve and celebrate the legacy of Lucy and Desi's work, but to enrich the world through 'THE HEALING POWER OF LAUGHTER'. Ewing also said any number of the 179 episodes is airing every day, somewhere around the world and heard in many different languages.

Ewing said, "While I think Lucy would have been thrilled that people are still watching her shows 60 years after its debut in 1951, I believe she would be happiest knowing that comedy was still such a part of people's lives. Lucy died at 77. Her daughter Lucie Arnez said her mother's show was about, "this childlike grown up who constantly gets into trouble, but at the end of the day, when she came home, there was someone waiting with unconditional love."

The Desilu Playhouse, the Lucy-Desi Museum and the Lucille Ball-Desi Arnez Center are popular tour points of interest in Jamestown, N.Y.

MEMORABLE QUOTES OF
'I LOVE LUCY' SHOWS 1961

Fred: She said my mother looks like a weasel
Lucy: Ethel, apologize
Ethel: I'm sorry your mother looks like a weasel

Lucy: It's seventy-nine cents a pound
Customer: How can you sell meat so cheap?
Lucy: I'm glad you asked that. We rope, we brand, we butcher. We do everything but eat it for you. Seventy-nine cents a pound.

Lucy: I want the names to be unique and euphonious
Ricky: Okay. Unique if it's a boy, and Euphonious if it's a girl.

Lucy: Ever since we said, "I do," there have been so many things that we don't.

(When Ethel doesn't return to California hotel suite)
Fred: Let's just hope for the best.
Lucy: Don't worry, Fred. Ethel will come back.
Fred: I said let's hope for the BEST.

Lucy: If some other woman were to take Fred away from you, you'd be singing a different tune, too.
Ethel: Yeah. "Happy Days are here again..."

Ricky: Lucy, you got some 'splainin' to do.

Ricky: What do you know about rice?
Fred: Well, I had it thrown at me on one of the darkest days in my life.

Ethel: Gee, this high altitude sure gives me an appetite.
Fred: What's your excuse at sea level?

Ethel: Imagine me meeting a Queen face to face. I'm scared.
Fred: You're scared? Think of the Queen?

Lucy: We have to find Sylvia Collins a husband, but where?
Ethel: I'll make the sacrifice, she can have mine.

Ethel: There's a lots of things you're good at.
Lucy: Like what?
Ethel: Well, you're awfully good at, uh, you're always been great at.

Lucy: Those are the same ones Ricky came up with.

Fred: We'll sue you.
Ricky: Yeah? We'll see who's gonna sue who.
Lucy: Yeah, we'll sue who's gonna see.

Ricky: Fred, I've got an awful problem on my hands
Fred: You should have thought about that before you married her.

Ricky: This whole thing is my fault. Something I said that started this whole mess.
Lucy: What's that?
Ricky: "I do".

(At a fake séance, introducing Ethel in disguise)
Lucy: This is Madam Ethel Mertzola. She'll be our Medium tonight. She's psychopathic.

Ethel: I refuse to go anywhere with someone who thinks I am a hippopotamus.
Ricky: Lucy, is this true?
Lucy: No. I just implied that she was a little hippy, thought she has got the biggest potamus I've ever seen.

(Lucy gets caught spying on the neighbors)
Lucy: I was uh...bird-watching!
Ricky: Bird-watching?
Lucy: Uh, yeah! Do you know that there's a yellow-bellied wood peck on our lawn?
Ricky: No, but I know that there's a red-headed cuckoo in the living room.

Those were the good ole days!

PART II

WHERE THE JOKES ARE
ENJOY!

CHAPTER I

KIDZ KORNER

Let's travel back in time when your children first learned the simple knock-knock jokes, the one-liners, and the chicken crossing the street puns. Remember the joy and excitement they felt that made them fall down with giggles and strange gurgling sounds of mirth? Come, step into the 'wee wit world' of fun and laughter and relive the The Kidz Korner.

ROLE PLAYING

A father returning from work one day heard his son and daughter quarreling violently with each other. "Children, why are you fighting so?" The little boy answered with an airy smile, "Why father, we aren't quarreling. We're just playing mother and father."

THE FIRST WEDDING

Dwayne witnessed his first wedding. After it was over, he asked his mother, "How many women can a man marry?" His mother asked, "Why do you ask, Dwayne?" He said, "Well I think it's 16, but the minister spoke of 'till death do us part'. In the ceremony, he said four better, four worse, four richer and four poorer. That's 16 Ma."

HE'S MY BROTHER

Two young boys walked into a pharmacy one day and picked up a box of tampons and went to the checkout counter.

The man at the counter asked the older boy, "Son, how old are you?" "Eight," the boy replied. The man continued, "Do you know what these are used for?"

The boy replied, "Not exactly, but they aren't for me. They're for him. He's my brother. We saw on TV that if you use these you would be able to swim and ride a bike. He can't do either."

MY DAD'S JOB

Three little boys were bragging about their fathers. One said, "My father only has to write a few words that they call a poem, and he is paid $50. The next little boy said, "Well, my father hums a few bars of music and they call it a song and he is paid $100. The third boy said, "My dad writes a few words and they call it a sermon and eight people are needed to collect all the money."

AMERICA'S SMARTEST WOMAN

A plane with four passengers is about to crash, but has only three parachutes. The first passenger says, "I'm Kobe Bryant, the best NBA player. The Lakers need me. I can't afford to die." So he takes the first parachute and leaves the plane.

The second passenger, Sarah Palin, says, "I was the running mate of the former Republican Party candidate for President of the United States. I am the most ambitious woman in the world. I am also a former Alaska Governor, a potential future President, and above all, the smartest women in America." She grabs the second parachute and leaves the plane.

The third passenger, the Rev. Billy Graham, says to the fourth passenger, a 10 year old school boy, "I am old and I don't have many years left. As a Christian I will sacrifice my life and let you have the last parachute."

The boy says, "It's okay. There is still a parachute left for you. America's smartest woman took my school backpack."

DADDY'S COMPUTER TALE

A little boy goes to his father and asks, "Daddy, how was I born?" The father answers, "Well, son, I guess one day you will need to find out anyway! Your mom and I first got together in a chat room on Yahoo. Then I set up a date via e-mail with your mom and we met at a cyber cafe. We sneaked into a secluded room and googled each other. There, your mother agreed to a download from my hard drive. As soon as I was ready to upload, we discovered that neither one of us had used a firewall, and since it was too late to hit the delete button, nine months later a little pop-up appeared that said: You Got Male!

HOW FAST THEY LEARN

NUDITY

I was driving with my three young children one warm summer evening when a woman in the convertible ahead of us stood up and waved. She was stark naked! As I was reeling from the shock, I heard my 5-year-old shout from the back seat, 'Mom, that lady isn't wearing a seat belt!'

OPINIONS

On the first day of school, a first-grader handed his teacher a note from his mother. The note read, *"The opinions expressed by this child are not necessarily those of his parents."*

KETCHUP

A woman was trying hard to get the ketchup out of the jar. During her struggle the phone rang so she asked her 4-year-old daughter to answer the phone. "Mommy can't come to the phone to talk to you right now. She's hitting the bottle."

MORE NUDITY

A little boy got lost at the YMCA and found himself in the women's locker room. When he was spotted, the room burst into shrieks, with ladies grabbing towels and running for cover. The little boy watched in amazement and then asked. "What's the matter, haven't you ever seen a little boy before?"

SCHOOL

A little girl had just finished her first week of school. "I'm just wasting my time," she said to her mother, "I can't read I can't write, and they won't let me talk!"

BIBLE

A little boy opened the big family Bible. He was fascinated as he fingered through the old pages. Suddenly, something fell out of the Bible. He picked up the object and looked at it.

What he saw was an old leaf that had been pressed in between the pages. "Mama, look what I found," the boy called out. "What have you got there, dear?" With astonishment in the young boy's voice, he answered, "I think it's Adam's underwear!"

OUT OF THE MOUTHS OF BABES

One day a little girl was sitting and watching her mother do the dishes at the kitchen sink. She suddenly noticed that her mother had several strands of white hair sticking out in contrast to her brunette hair.

She looked at her mother and inquisitively asked, "Why are some of your hairs white, Mom?" Her mother replied, "Well, every time that you do something wrong and make me cry or unhappy, one of my hairs turns white."

The little girl thought about this revelation for a while and then said, "Momma, how come ALL of grandma's hairs are white?"

SHIRLEY & MARCY

A mother was concerned about her kindergarten son walking to school. He didn't want his mother to walk with him. She wanted to give him the feeling that he had some independence but yet know that he was safe. So she had an idea of how to handle it.

She asked a neighbor if she would please follow him to school in the mornings, staying at a distance, so he probably wouldn't notice her. She said that since she was up early with her toddler anyway, it would be a good way for them to get some exercise as well, so she agreed.

The next school day, the neighbor and her little girl set out following behind Timmy as he walked to school with another neighbor girl he knew. She did this for the whole week.

As the two walked and chatted, kicking stones and twigs, Timmy's little friend noticed the same lady was following them as she seemed to do every day all week. Finally, she said to Timmy, "Have you noticed that lady following us to school all week? Do you know her?"

Timmy nonchalantly replied, "Yeah, I know who she is." The little girl said, "Well, who is she?" "That's just Shirley Goodnest," Timmy replied. "And her daughter, Marcy."

"Shirley Goodnest?" Who is she and why is she following us?" "Well," Timmy explained, "every night my Mom makes me say the 23rd Psalm with my prayers 'cuz she worries about me so much. And in the Psalm, it says, 'Shirley Goodnest and Marcy shall follow me all the days of my life'. so I guess I'll just have to get used to it."

"The Lord bless you and keep you: the Lord make His face to shine upon you, and be gracious unto you; the Lord lift His countenance upon you, and give you peace. May Shirley Goodnest and Marcy be with you today and always."

A MILLION DOLLAR RESCUE

On one of the premier cruise ships, a five year old Boy fell overboard. The father of the boy began screaming, "Save my child. Save my boy, some one. I will give them a million dollars to save my boy." Suddenly, a white haired 80 year old gentleman flies overboard, swims to the child, and rescues the boy. The father cried his thanks to the man and promises to give him the million dollars. The old man said, "I got my own money, I don't need it. I'm in good shape. But would someone tell me who pushed me?"

ABSENT MOTHER

Danny and Allen were taking a trip down memory lane. Danny said, "Brother, do you remember when Mother took us on our first cruise to the Bahamas?" Allen replied, "How could I forget that trip? It took us three days before we realized that Ma was on another boat."

"Did you know that laughter is an instant vacation?"

Milton Berle

KIDDIES ON MOMMIES

All answers given by 2nd grade school children:

Q.   Why did God make Mothers?

- She's the only one who knows where the Scotch Tape is.//
- Mostly to clean the house.
- To help us out of there when we were getting born.

Q.   How did God make Mothers?

- Magic, plus super powers and a lot of stirring.
- He used dirt, just like for the rest of us.
- God made my mom just the same like he made me. He just used bigger parts.

Q.   If you could change one thing about your Mom, what would it be?

- She has this weird thing about me keeping my room clean. I'd get rid of that.

- I'd make my Mom smarter. Then, she would know it was my sister who did it, not me.

- I would like for her to get rid of the those invisible eyes on the back of her head.

Q. What ingredients are Mothers made of?

- God makes mothers out of clouds and Angel hair and everything nice in the world and one dab of mean.

- They had to get their start from men's bones. Then they mostly use string, I think.

Q. What kind of a little girl was your Mom?

- My Mom has always been my Mom and none of that other stuff.

- I don't know because I wasn't there, but my guess would be pretty bossy.

- They say she used to be nice.

Q. What did your Mom need to know about Dad before she married him?

- His last name.

- She had to know his background. Like is he a crook? Does he get drunk on beer?

- Does he make at least $800 a year? Did he say No to drugs and Yes to chores?

Q. Why did your Mom marry your Dad?

- My Dad makes the best spaghetti in the world. And my Mom eats a lot.

- She got too old to do anything else with him.

- My grandma says that Mom didn't have her thinking cap on.

Q Who is the boss at your house?

- Mom doesn't want to be boss, but she has to because Dad's such a goof ball.

- Mom. You can tell by room inspection. She sees the stuff under the bed.

- I guess Mom is, but only because she has a lot more to do than Dad.

Q.   What would it take to make your Mom perfect?

- On the inside she's already perfect. Outside, I think some kind of plastic surgery.

- Diet. You know her hair I'd diet, maybe blue.

PLAYING 'JESUS'

A mother was preparing pancakes for her sons, Kevin 5, and Ryan 3. The boys began to argue over who would get the first pancake. Their mother saw the opportunity for a moral lesson. She asked, "If Jesus were sitting here, what would He say?" "Let my brother have the first pancake, I can wait." Kevin turned to his younger brother and say, "Ryan, you be Jesus."

ASK THE RIGHT QUESTION

There was this little boy and a big dog sitting by him on the steps. A man was passing by and asked the boy, "does your dog bite?" The boy said, "No." The man reached down to pet the dog and the dog bit half his arm off. the man said, "I thought you said your dog didn't bite?" The boy replied, "He's not mine."

LARGE SIGN POSTED IN A RESTAURANT

We love kids, but please keep yours at your table! Unattended kids will be given a shot of espresso and a free puppy.

Signed The Owner.

TIMMIE'S LEARNING

Timmie meets his grandmother for the first time. After staring at her for a minute, he asks, "Grandma are you considered an antique?"

FROM BILL COSBY'S REMAKE OF ART LINKLETTER'S "KIDS SAY THE DARNDEST THINGS":

Cosby: What would you like to be when you grow up?

Kid: An airplane pilot.

Cosby: So, what would you do if your plane ran out of gas?

Kid: I'd parachute out of the plane and go get gas.

Cosby: Well, what about your passengers?

Kid: I'll tell 'em, "I'll be right back."

GOD IS WATCHING

The children were lined up in the cafeteria of a Catholic school for lunch. At the head of the table was a large pile of apples. The Nun made a note and posted on the tray. It read, "Take only one. God is watching." Moving further along the lunch line was a large pile of chocolate chip cookies. One child whispered to another, "Take all you want. God is watching the apples."

THEY COME HERE SMART

Little girl: When I get to heaven, I am going to ask Jonah if he really was swallowed by a whale.

Teacher: What if Jonah wasn't in heaven and God told you that poor Jonah misbehaved and he was in hell?

Little girl: Well then, Ms. Richardson, you can ask him.

SAYING GRACE IN A RESTAURANT

Sometimes we forget the really important things in life. Last week, I took my grand-child to a restaurant. My six-year-old grandson asked if he could say grace. As we bowed our heads he said, "God is good, God is great. Thank you for the food, and I would even thank you more if Nana gets us ice cream for dessert. And liberty and justice for all! Amen!"

Along with the laughter from the other customers nearby, I heard a woman remark, "That's what's wrong with this country. Kids today don't even know how to pray. Asking God for ice cream! Why, I never!"

Hearing this, my grandson burst into tears and asked me, "Did I do it wrong? Is God mad at me?"

As I held him and assured him that he had done a terrific job, and God was certainly not mad at him, an elderly gentleman approached the table; He winked at my grandson and said, "I happen to know that God thought that was a great prayer." "Really?" my grandson asked. "Cross my heart," the man replied.

Then, in a theatrical whisper, he added (indicating the woman whose remark had started this whole thing), "Too bad she never asks God for ice cream. A little ice cream is good for the soul sometimes."

Naturally, I bought my grandchildren ice cream at the end of the meal. My grandson stared at his for a moment, and then did something I will remember the rest of my life.

My grandson picked up his bowl of ice cream and placed it before the disgruntled lady and sweetly said to her, "Here, this is for you. Ice cream is good for the soul, sometimes; and my soul is good already."

LESLIE AND BERNICE FLYNN'S JOKES ON DISCIPLINE OF CHILDREN

Two fathers were discussing the problems of raising families. One asked, "Do you strike your kids?" Only in self-defense, came the answer.

A mother was trying to explain the meaning of grandfather and grandmother. "Now if grandfather is my father, can you tell me who grandmother is?" "Sure," replied the girl. "Grandmother is the white-haired lady who keeps you from spanking me."

A little boy was picking up his toys and tidying his room. His playmate said, "Oh, I see you're straightening up your room. I guess your Mom is going to give you something if you clean it all up nice?" "Oh no," retorted the boy. "She's going to give me something if I don't clean things up."

The department store was crowded with shoppers. A young mother had the added difficulty of a small daughter pulling and tugging at her side, and whimpering incessantly.

Suddenly, the harassed mother pleaded softly, "Quiet. Susanna, just calm yourself and take it easy," an admiring clerk commented on the mother's psychology, then turned to the child. "So your name is Susanna?" "Oh no," said the mother. "Her name is Joan, I'm Susanna."

WALMART - THE RETAILER?

Pastor Osteen recalled a story about a neighbor mowing her lawn, when suddenly her cat screamed. She ran to the bushes and there she found her poor cat bleeding profusely with its tail cut off. After crying and begging for help, her 10-year-old son came outside with a big bath towel, and wrapped kitty and his tail up and started running to the car saying, "Ma, come drive us to the Wal-Mart. The mother said to her son, "What makes you think we can get kitty some help at Wal-Mart? Her son said, "Ma, isn't Wal-Mart the world's largest RE-tailer?"

WHERE'S GOD

A Sunday school teacher of preschoolers was concerned that his student might be a little confused about Jesus Christ because of the Christmas season emphasis on His birth. He wanted to make sure they understood that the birth of Jesus occurred for real. He asked his class, "Where is Jesus today?" Steven raised his hand and said, "He's in heaven." Mary was called on and answered, "He's in my heart." Little Johnny, waving his hand furiously, blurted out, "I know, I know! He's in our bathroom! The whole class got very quiet, looked at the teacher, and waited for a response. The teacher was completely at a loss for a few very long seconds. Finally, he gathered his wits and asked Little Johnny how he knew this. Little Johnny said, "Well, every morning, my father gets up, bangs on the bathroom door, and yells, "Good Lord, are you still in there!"

FUNNIEST KIDS JOKES

Q: What are the four seasons?

A: Salt, Pepper, Ketchup, Ranch

Q: Why are chefs hard to like?

A: Because they beat eggs, whip cream, and mash potatoes!

Q: Where do burgers like to dance?

A: At a Meatball!

Q: What kind of food is crazy about money?

A: A dough-nut!

Q: Why does Peter Pan always fly?

A: Because he can 'Neverland'.

Q: What do you call a piece of wood with nothing to do?

A: Bored - (Board)

Q: Why did the gardener plant his money?

A: He wanted the soil to be rich.

Q: Why is Cinderella so bad at sports?

A: Because she has a pumpkin for a coach, and she runs away from the ball.

Q: What did one angel say to the other angel?

A: Halo

Q: What did Cinderella say when her photos weren't ready?

A: "Someday my prints will come."

BEER BY SEVEN YEAR OLDS

A handful of 7-year-old children were asked, what they thought of beer. Some interesting responses, but this one is especially touching.

'I think beer must be good. My dad says the more beer he drinks the prettier my mom gets.' - Tim, 7 years old.

'Beer makes my dad sleepy and we get to watch what we want on television when he is asleep, so beer is nice. - Melanic, 7-years-old.

'My mom and dad both like beer. My mom gets funny when she drinks it and takes her top off at parties, but dad doesn't think this is very funny.' - Grady, 7 years old.

'My mom and dad talk funny when they drink beer and the more they drink the more they give kisses to each other, which is a good thing.' - Toby, 7-years old.

'My dad gets funny on beer. He is funny. He also wets his pants sometimes, so he shouldn't have too much.' - Sarah, 7 years-old.

'My dad loves beer. The more he drinks, the better he dances. One time he danced right into the pool.' - Lilly, 7 years old.

'I don't like beer very much. Every time Dad drinks it, he burns the sausages on the barbecue and they taste disgusting,' - Ethan, 7 years old.

'I give Dad's beer to the dog and he goes to sleep.' - Shirley, 7 years old.

'My mom drinks beer and she says silly things and picks on my father. Whenever she drinks beer she yells at Dad and tells him to go bury his bone down the street again. But that doesn't make any sense.' -

"Our Father, who does art in heaven, Harold is his name." Amen

Reese, 3 years old.

POLICE

It was the end of the day when I parked my police van in front of the station. As I gathered my equipment my K-9 partner Jake, was barking and I saw a little boy staring in at me. "Is that a dog you got back there?" He asked. "It sure is," I replied. Puzzled, the boy looked at me and then toward the back of the van. Finally, he asked, "What'd he do?"

NICE JOHNNIE

A new teacher was trying to make use of her psychology course so she started her class by saying: "Everyone who thinks they're stupid, standup!" After a few seconds, Little Johnny stood up. The teacher asked: "Do you think you're stupid little Johnny?" No ma'am he replied: "I hate to see you standing there all by yourself!"

IMPORTANCE: HIGH

Maybe there actually is some reason to admire the postal service.

It is not known who replied, but there is a beautiful soul working in the dead letter office of the US postal service.

Our 14 year old dog, Abbey, died last month. the day after she died, my 4 year old daughter Meredith was crying and talking about how much she missed Abbey. She asked if we could write a letter to God so that when Abbey got to heaven, God would recognize her. I told her that I thought we could, so she dictated these words:

Dear God,

Will you please take care of my dog? She died yesterday and is with you in heaven. I miss her very much. I am happy that you let me have her as my dog even though she got sick. I hope you will play with her. She likes to play with balls and to swim. I am sending a picture of her so when you see her you will know that she is my dog. I really miss her.   *Love Meredith*

We put the letter in an envelope with a picture of Abbey and Meredith and addressed it to God/Heaven. We put our return address on it. Then Meredith pasted several stamps on the front of the envelope because she said it would take lots of stamps to get the letter all the way to heaven. That afternoon she dropped it into the letter box at the post office. A few days later, she asked if God had gotten the letter yet. I told her that I thought he had.

Yesterday, there was a package wrapped in gold paper on our front porch addressed, 'To Meredith' in an unfamiliar hand. Meredith opened it. Inside was a book by Mr. Rogers called, 'When a Pet Dies…' Taped to the inside front cover was the letter we had written to God in its opened envelope. On the opposite page was the picture of Abbey & Meredith and this note:

Dear Meredith:

Abbey arrived safely in heaven. Having the picture was a big help. I recognized Abbey right away. Abbey isn't sick anymore. Her spirit is with me just like it stays in your heart.

Abbey loved being your dog. Since we don't need our bodies in Heaven and I don't have any pockets to keep your picture in, I am sending it back to you so you will have something to remember Abbey with.

Thank you for the loving letter and thank your mother for helping you write it and sending it to me. What a wonderful mother you have. I picked her especially for you. I send my blessings every day and remember that I love you very much. By the way, I am easy to find, I am wherever there is love.

CHAPTER II

ADULT JOKES

A wife invited some people to dinner. At the table she turned to her six year old daughter and said, "Would you like to say the blessing? The child replied, "I don't know what to say." just say what you hear me say." The child bowed her head and said, "Lord why on earth did I invite these people to dinner?"

HOW TO GET A QUICK RESPONSE FROM THE POLICE

George Phillips, from Meridian, Mississippi, was going up to bed, when his wife told him that he'd left the light on in the garden shed. George opened the back door to go turn it off, but saw that there were guys in the shed stealing things.

He phoned the police, who asked, "Is someone in your house?" He said, "No, but some people are breaking into my garden shed and stealing from me."

Then the police dispatcher said, "All patrols are busy. You should lock your doors and an officer will be long when one is available." George said okay. He hung up the phone and counted to 30. Then he phoned the police again.

"Hello, I just called you a few seconds ago because there were people stealing things from my shed. Well, you don't have to worry about them now, because I just shot and killed them both. The dogs are eating them right now." and he hung up.

Within five minutes, six police cars, a SWAT Team, a helicopter, two fire trucks, a paramedic and an ambulance showed up at the Phillips' residence, and caught the burglars red-handed.

One of the policemen said to George, "I thought you said that you'd shot them!" George said, "I thought you said there was nobody available!"

TANKS FOR THE MEMORIES

As a bagpiper, I play many gigs. Recently, I was asked by a funeral director to play at a graveside service for a homeless man. He had no family or friends, so the service was held at a pauper's cemetery.

Being unfamiliar with the area, I got lost; after wandering for an hour, I finally arrived an hour late, and saw the funeral was evidently over and the hearse nowhere in sight.

There were only the diggers and crew left and they were eating lunch. I felt badly and apologized to the men for being late, then went to the side of the grave and looked down.

The vault lid was already in place. I didn't know what else to do, so I started to play.

The workers put down their lunches and began to gather around. I played out my heart and soul for this man with no family and friends. I played like I've never played before.

As I played, Amazing Grace, the workers began to weep. They wept, I wept, we all wept together. When I finished I packed up my bagpipes and started for my car. Though my head hung low, my heart was full.

"Sweet mother of Jesus! I never seen nothin' like that before and I've been putting in septic tanks for 20 years," one of the workers said.

By Michael Cooke

WHY MEN ARE NEVER DEPRESSED

Men are just happier people.

Your last name stays put.

The garage is all yours.

Wedding plans take care of themselves.

Chocolate is just another snack.

You can never be pregnant.

Car mechanics tell you the truth.

The world is your urinal.

You never have to drive to another petrol station restroom because this one is just too icky.

You don't have to stop and think of which way to turn a nut on a bolt.

Same work, more pay.

Wrinkles add character.

People never stare at your chest when you're talking to them.

New shoes don't cut, blister, or mangle your feet.

One mood all the time.

Phone conversations are over in 30 seconds flat.

You know stuff about tanks and engines.

A ten-day vacation requires only one suitcase.

You can open all your own jars.

You get extra credit for the slightest act of thoughtfulness.

BOOTS

Did you hear about the teacher who was helping one of her kindergarten students put on his boots?

He asked for help and she could see why. With her pulling and him pushing, the boots still didn't want to go on. When the second boot was on, she had worked up a sweat. She almost whimpered when the little boy said, "Teacher, they're on the wrong feet." She looked and sure enough, they were.

It wasn't any easier pulling the boots off than it was putting them on. She managed to keep her cool as together they worked to get the boots back on, this time on the right feet. He then announced, "These aren't my boots."

She bit her tongue rather than get right in his face and scream, "Why didn't you say so?" Like she wanted to.

Once again she struggled to help him pull the ill-fitting boots off. He then said, "They're my brother's boots. My Mom made me wear them."

She didn't know if she should laugh or cry. She mustered up the grace and courage she had left to wrestle the boots on his feet again. She said, "Now, where are your mittens?"

He said, I stuffed them in the toes of my boots…"

Her trial starts next month.

A MOTHERS CURSE

A woman gets on the bus with her baby. The bus driver says, "That's the ugliest baby that I've ever seen Ugh!" The woman goes to the rear of the bus and sits down frowning. She says to a man next to her, "That driver just insulted me!" The man says, "You go right back up there and tell him. Go ahead. I'll hold your monkey for you."

HE'S REALLY GOT A DRINKING PROBLEM

Two guys are sitting on a bar stool. One starts to insult the other one. He screams, "I slept with your mother!" The bar gets very quiet as everyone listens to see what the other weasel will do. The first guy yells again, "I slept with your mother!" The other says, "Go home Dad. You're drunk."

IDIOT SIGHTINGS

The stoplight on the corner buzzes when it's safe to cross the street. I was crossing with an intellectually challenged coworker of mine. She asked if I knew what the buzzer was for. I explained that it signals blind people when the light is red. Appalled, she responded, "What on earth are blind people doing driving?" She was a probation officer in Wichita, KS.

GIVING UP WINE

I was walking down the street when I was accosted by a particularly dirty, shabby looking, homeless woman who asked me for a couple of dollars for dinner. I took out my wallet, got out ten dollars and asked, "If I give you this money will you buy wine with it instead of dinner?"

"No, I had to stop drinking years ago," the homeless woman told me. "Will you use it to go shopping instead of buying food?" I asked.

"No, I don't waste time shopping,' the homeless woman said, 'I need to spend all my time trying to stay alive."

"Will you spend this on a beauty salon instead of food?" I asked. "Are you nuts lady? I haven't had my hair done in 20 years." "Well," I said, "I'm not going to give you the money. Instead, I m going to take you out for dinner with my husband and me." The homeless woman was shocked. "Won't your husband be furious with you for doing that? I know I'm dirty, and I probably smell pretty bad."

I said, "That's okay. It's important for him to see what a woman looks like after she has given up shopping, hair appointments, and wine."

LAST RESPECTS

At a motivational seminar three men are asked to come up to the stage.

They are all asked, "When you are in your casket and friends and family are mourning you, what would you like to hear them say.

The first guy says, "I would like to hear them say that I was the great doctor of my time, and a great family man."

The second guy says, "I would like to hear that I was wonderful husband and school teacher who made a huge difference in our children of tomorrow."

The last guy replies, "I would like to hear them say. LOOK!!! HE'S MOVING!!!"

WELFARE CLIENT

A guy walks into the local welfare office, marches straight up to the counter and says, "Hi, You know, I just HATE drawing welfare. I'd really rather have a job."

The social worker behind the counter says, "Your timing is excellent. We just got a job opening from a very wealthy old man who wants a chauffeur/bodyguard for his nymphomaniac daughter. You'll have to drive around in his Mercedes, but he'll supply all of your clothes. Because of the long hours, meals will be provided.

You'll be expected to escort her on her overseas holiday trips. You will have to satisfy her sexual urges. You'll have a two bedroom apartment above the garage. The starting salary is $200,000 a year."

The guy asks, "Are you jerking my chain?" The social worker says, "Yeah, well, you started it."

COLD AND DEEP

Richard Pryor was one of the country's funniest comedians a couple decades ago, his material, however, was known to be quite "blue". This joke was considered to be in the "one upmanship' genre, or "man's bragging rights."

After a long night of drinking, brother Josef and his cousin James left the bar to go home. Stumbling down the street they approached the town's bridge. Proceeding to cross, they barely reached the middle when nature insisted on calling on both men. After a sigh of relief, James said, "Bro, this water sure is cold." Josef stuttered and said, "Yeah and it sure is deep too."

SECRETS TO A LONG HAPPY MARRIAGE

An old woman was sipping on a glass of wine while sitting on the patio with her husband and she says, "I love you so much. I don't know how I could ever live without you." Her husband asks, "Is that you, or the wine talking?" She replies, "It's me talking to the wine."

AN ELDERLY FLORIDIAN

An elderly Floridian called 911 on her cell phone to report that her car has been broken into. She is hysterical as she explains her situation to the dispatcher. "They've stolen the stereo, the steering wheel, the brake pedal and even the accelerator!" she cried. The dispatcher said, "Stay calm. An officer is on the way."

A few minutes later, the officer radios in. "Disregard," he says. "She got in the back seat by mistake."

WHAT A CHOICE

A little old lady was running up and down the halls in a nursing home. As she walked, she would flip up the hem of her nightgown and say, "Supersex." She walked up to an elderly man in a wheelchair. Flipping her gown at him, she said, "Supersex."

He sat silently for a moment or two and finally answered, "I'll take the soup."

WHAT'S YOUR NAME, AGAIN?

Two elderly ladies had been friends for many decades. Over the years they had shared all kinds of activities and adventures. Lately, their activities had been limited to playing cards a few times a week. One day, when playing cards, one looked at the other and said, "Now don't get mad at me. I know we've been friends a long time, but I just can't think of your name. I've thought and thought, but I can't remember it. Please tell me what your name is."

Her friend glared at her. For at least three minutes she just stared and glared. Finally, she said, "How soon do you need to know?"

HARD OF HEARING

Morris, an 82-year-old man, went to the doctor to get a physical. A few days later the doctor saw Morris walking down the street with a gorgeous young lady on his arm. A couple of days later, the doctor spoke to Morris and said, "you're really doing great, aren't you? Morris replied, "Just doing what you said, doctor. 'Get a hot mamma and be cheerful.' The doctor said, "I didn't say that. I said you got a heart mummer and be careful."

OLD WISDOM

After working his farm every day, an old farmer rarely had time to enjoy the large pond in the back that he had fixed up earlier with picnic tables, horseshoe courts and benches.

So one evening he decided to go down and see how things were holding up. Much to his surprise, he heard voices shouting and laughing with glee. As he came closer he saw it was a group of young women skinny dipping in his pond. He made the women aware of his presence and they screamed and splashed their way down to the deep end. One of the ladies shouted to him, "We're not coming out until you leave." The old farmer replied, "I didn't come down here to watch you ladies swim or make you get out of the pond naked. I only came down to feed the alligator." MORAL: Old age and treachery will always triumph over youth and skill.

HOW WE DO IT AT OSCAR'S FUNERAL PARLOR

An old lady was very upset because her husband Albert had just passed away. She went to the undertakers to have one last look at her dearly departed husband. The instant she saw him she started crying. The mortician walked over to comfort her.

Through her tears she explained that she was upset because Albert was wearing a black suit, and it was his fervent wish to be buried in a blue suit.

The mortician apologized and explained that traditionally, they always put bodies in a black suit, but he'll see what he could arrange. The next day she returned to the funeral parlor to have one last moment with Albert before the funeral the following day. When the mortician pulled back the curtain, she managed a smile through her tears as Albert was resplendent in a smart blue suit.

"Wonderful, but where did you get that beautiful suit?" "Well, yesterday afternoon, after you left, a man about your husband's size was brought in and he was wearing a blue suit. His wife was quite upset because she wanted him buried in the traditional black suit." Albert's wife smiled at the undertaker. "After that," he continued, it was just a matter of swapping heads."

ADAM ... GOD'S ROUGH DRAFT

God said: Adam, I want you to do something for me.

Adam said: Gladly, Lord, what do you want me to do?

God said: Go down into that valley.

Adam said: What's a valley? God explained it to him.

Then God said: Cross the river.

Adam said: What's a river?

God explained that to him and then said, "Go over the hill."

Adam said: What is a hill?

So, God explained to Adam what a hill was. He told Adam, on the other side of the hill you will find a cave.

Adam said: What's a cave?

After God explained, he added, in the cave you will find a woman.

Adam said: What's a woman?

So God explained that to him too.

God said: I want you to reproduce.

Adam said: How do I do that?

God first said (under his breath): GEEZ! and then, just like everything else, God explained.

So, Adam goes down into the valley, across the river, and over the hill into the cave, and finds the woman.

Then in about five minutes, he was back. God, whose patience was wearing thin said angrily: What now Adam?

And Adam said: What's a headache?

CHAPTER III

CHURCH JOKES

GIMME THAT OLE TIME RELIGION

Why is it that the vivid memories of our small community churches and their unique form of worship, can energize us like nothing else can? Where deacons, ushers, choir members and our ministers could provide us with "cover your mouth humor and church ladies, their big hat and fat-ladden chicken dinners were unforgettable.

Do you remember the life lessons of growth where you earned a string of titles for your volunteerism and free-will offerings? It was there you learned how to sing, praise-dance and developed the ability to memorize those long recitations and quote pages of bible verses? Yes, the church was the center of our community activities and the beginning of our social life. Now in Chapter III, you will enjoy humor of the funniest kind. So go on, Laugh Again and Again.

TRYING TO FIND JESUS

One Sunday morning, Tom, the town's drunk was walking along the road where he heard some singing and screaming, so he followed the sounds to the creek. Here he saw a lot of people in white sheets and the minister was baptizing them. The minister looked up and saw Tom, and invited him to come join them.

Tom said, "Why not. Yes Pastor Jones. I'll join you." After a few bars of Shall We Gather by the River, the minister grabs Tom and dipped him in the creek.

The minister said, "Tom, did you see Jesus?" Tom said, "No, pastor." The minister grabbed him again and this time held him down a little longer. When he came up the minister asked him again, "Tom, did you see Jesus?" Tom said, "No." So, Pastor Jones thought a moment and this time he grabbed Tom and held him down a full minute and this time he said, "Tom I know you saw Jesus this time didn't you?"

And the man stood up shook his head and said, "Pastor Jones, are you sure this is where Jesus went down?"

I'M A WITNESS

There was a knock on my door this morning. I opened it to find a young man standing there who said: "Hello sir, I'm a Jehovah's Witness."

I said, "Come in and sit down." I offered him coffee and asked, "What do you want to talk about?" He said, "Beats the crap out of me. I've never gotten this far before."

SPECIAL PRAYER FOR LEROY

Leroy was one of the young men who attended church only when he was in trouble. On this particular Wednesday, when the preacher asked, "Anyone with needs to be prayed over, come forward to the alter." Leroy got in line.

When it was his turn, the preacher asks, "Leroy what do you want me to pray about this evening?" Leroy replied, "Pray for my hearing, Pastor." So, Pastor Jones put one of his hands over Leroy's ear, and the other hand on his head, and he prayed long, loud and powerfully. Then he said, "Leroy can you hear now?" Leroy said, "I won't know 'til next Wednesday, Pastor. That's when my hearing is."

RESSURECTION STORY

Pastor Joel Osteen told this one in Jerusalem where he was the guest speaker on a program entitled, "An Evening of Hope & Inspiration."

A man's wife died while they were vacationing in Jerusalem. Seeking help from an official to make arrangements to take his wife's body back to the states, he was explained the procedures. Costs were discussed and he was told that it would cost $5,000 to send the body to America, but only $100 if he could bury her in Jerusalem. After a little thinking he said, "I've decided to take my wife's body home with me. It's not a money problem it's because I remember being told the story about a man who died and was buried here, and he arose in three days. I best make my own arrangements.

Pope John Paul II was attributed to have said to a couple preparing for marriage that, "Anyone who loves is closer to God than they think."

Chicago Catholic News.

NEW CHURCH SIGNS

The Best Vitamin for a Christian is B1

Try Our Sunday...It's Better than Baskin-Robbins.

Come In and Have Your FAITH LIFTED.

Can't Sleep? Try Counting Your Blessings.

Try Jesus. If you don't like him, the devil will always take you back.

ASPIRE TO INSPIRE BEFORE YOU EXPIRE

Where will you be sitting in Eternity? Smoking or Non-Smoking?

Under Same Management for Over 2,000 Years.

THOSE WONDERFUL CHURCH BULLETINS

I couldn't resist sharing some Christian Church humor found in the bulletins and announcements passed out at their services. These sentences actually appeared. I did not, "airbrushed them".

The Fasting & Prayer Conference will be held first Saturday in February. It will include meals.

The Sermon this morning: "Jesus Walks on the Water."

The Sermon tonight: "Searching for Jesus."

Please place your donation in the envelope along with the deceased person you want remembered.

The church will host an evening of fine dining, super entertainment and gracious hostility.

Potluck supper Sunday at 5:00 PM - prayer and medication to follow.

The ladies of the church have cast off clothing of every kind. They may be seen in the basement on Friday afternoon.

This evening at 7 PM there will be a hymn singing in the park across from the Church, Bring a blanket and come prepared to sin.

Ladies Bible Study will be held Thursday morning at 10AM. All ladies are invited to lunch in the Fellowship Hall after the B.S. is done.

The pastor would appreciate it if the ladies of the congregation would lend him their electric girdles for the pancake breakfast next Sunday.

Low Self Esteem Support Group will meet Thursday at 7 PM. Please use the back door.

The eight-graders will be presenting Shakespeare's Hamlet in the Church' basement Friday at 7 PM. The congregation is invited to attend this tragedy.

Weight Watchers will meet at 7 PM at the First Presbyterian Church. Please use large double doors at the side entrance.

The Associate Minister unveiled the church's new tithing campaign slogan last Sunday: "I Upped My Pledge...Up Yours!"

LIKE GEORGE. THEY DID NOT TELL A LIE

At the end of the Age, when all the Believers were standing in line to get into heaven, God appeared and said, "I want all the men to form two lines. One line will be for the men who were the true heads of their households. The other will be for the men who were dominated by their wives."

God continued: "I want all the women to report to St. Peter."

The women left and the men formed two lines. The line of men who were dominated by their wives was seemingly unending. The line of men who were the true head of their household had one man in it.

God said to the first line: You men ought to be ashamed of yourselves. I appointed you to be the head of your households and you were disobedient and have not fulfilled your purpose. Of all of you, there is only one man who obeyed me. Learn from him."

Then God turned to the lone man and asked, "How did you come to be in this line?" The man replied, *"My wife told me to stand here."*

****

Money isn't everything, but it sure keeps the kid's in touch.

One good thing about Alzheimer's is you get to meet new people every day.

Xerox and Wurlitzer will merge to produce reproductive organs.

Do not ask God to guide your footsteps if you are not willing to move your feet.

FAVORITE OLD JOKES FROM ACULEUS

While robbing a home, a burglar hears someone say, "Jesus is watching you." To his relief, he realizes that it's only a parrot mimicking something he had heard. The burglar asked the parrot? What's your name? The parrot answered, "Moses."

The burglar goes on to comment, "What kind of a person names their parrot Moses?" The parrot replies, "The same kind of person who names his Rottweiler, Jesus?"

SHE WAS A GOOD WIFE

As a funeral train passes by a golf course, a golfer on the greens stops, stands at attention with hat held over his heart as the hearse goes by. Then he goes back to lining up his putt. His playing partner remarked how that was the nicest gesture he's ever seen -- to show such respect for the dead. The first golfer sinks his putt and says, "Well, she was a very good wife for 16 years."

HYMNS FOR THE OVER 50

- GIVE ME THE OLD TIMERS RELIGION
- PRECIOUS LORD, TAKE MY HAND, AND HELP ME UP
- JUST A SLOWER WALK WITH THEE
- GO TELL IT ON THE MOUNTAIN, BUT SPEAK LOUDER
- NOBODY KNOWS THE TROUBLE I HAVE SEEING
- GUIDE ME O THOU GREAT LORD GOD, I'VE FORGOTTEN WHERE I'VE PARKED THE CAR
- COUNT YOUR MANY BIRTHDAYS, COUNT THEM ONE BY ONE
- BLESSED INSURANCE
- IT IS WELL WITH MY SOUL, BUT MY KNEES HURT

HOW TO GET THE QUESTION ANSWERED

There was a lady who had to do a lot traveling for her business. Flying was a necessity which made her very nervous, so she always took her Bible along to read and it helped to relax her.

One trip she was sitting next to a man who watched her pull out her Bible. He gave a little chuckle and went back to what he was reading.

After a while, he turned to her and asked, "You don't really believe all that stuff in there, do you? The lady replied, "Of course I do. It is the Bible, after all." The man said, "Well, what about that guy that was swallowed by the whale?" She replied, "Oh Jonah. Yes, I believe that it is in the Bible." He asked, "Well, how do you suppose he survived all that time inside the whale?" The lady said, "Well, I don't really know. I guess when I get to heaven, I will ask him." What if he isn't in heaven?" The man said sarcastically. "Then, you can ask him," she replied.

What do you see when you wake up in the morning and look in the mirror? A motivated, happy person or an unhappy, confused, lonely one?

"Henry David Thoreau said, "The question is not what you look at, but what you see."

CHURCH GOSSIP

Mildred, the church gossip and self-appointed arbiter of the church's morals, kept sticking her nose in the other members' private lives. Church members were unappreciative of her activities, but feared her enough to maintain their silence.

She made a mistake, however, when she accused George, a new member, of being an alcoholic after she saw his pickup truck parked in front of the town's only bar one afternoon.

She commented to George and others that everyone seeing it there would know what he was doing.

George, a man of few words, stared at her for a moment and just walked away. He didn't explain, defend, or deny. He said nothing.

Later that evening, George quietly parked his pickup in front of Mildred's house and left it there all night!

THE CLEANING WOMAN

There was a little old cleaning woman that went to the local church when the invitation was given at the end of the service she went forward wanting to become a member. The pastor listened as she told him how she had accepted Jesus and wanted to be baptized and become a member of the church.

The pastor thought to himself, "Oh my, she is so unkempt, even smells as little, and her fingernails are not clean. She picks up garbage, cleans toilets - what would the members think of her," He told her that she needed to go home and pray about it and then decide.

The following week, here she came again. She told the pastor that she had prayed about it and still wanted to be baptized.

"I have passed this church for so long. It is so beautiful, and I truly want to become a member."

Again, the pastor told her to go home and pray some more. A few weeks later while out eating at the restaurant, the pastor saw the little old lady.

He did not want her to think that he was ignoring her so he approached her and said, "I have not seen you for a while. Is everything all right?"

"Oh, yes," she said. "I talked with Jesus, and he told me not to worry about becoming a member of your church."

"He did?" said the pastor.

"Oh yes," she replied. "He said even he hasn't been able to get into your church yet and he's been trying for years."

TOP JOKE IN NORTHERN IRELAND

A doctor says to his middle-aged patient, "I have bad news and worse news." "Oh dear, what's the bad news?" asked the patient. The doctor replies, "You only have 24 hours to live." "That's terrible," said the patient. "How can the news possibly be worse?" The doctor replies, "I've been trying to contact you since yesterday."

Blessed are they who can laugh at themselves for they shall never ceased to be amused.   *Joachins Verbagan*

CHAPTER IV

CORPORATE HUMOR

Someone once said the world is being governed by former C students. Of course, there are always exceptions to this kind of combative ideology. In Chapter IV, corporate and business activities are looked upon comically. I think you might agree that some of the so-called leaders at the helm can "make ya wanna holla!"

THE MATERIALISTIC LAWYER

A very successful lawyer parked his brand-new Mercedes in front of his office, ready to show it off to his colleagues. As he got out, a truck passed too close and completely tore off the door on the driver's side. The lawyer immediately grabbed his cell phone, dialed 911, and within minutes a policeman pulled up. Before the officer has a chance to ask any questions, the lawyer started screaming hysterically. His Mercedes, which he had just picked up the day before, was now completely ruined and would never be the same, no matter what the body shop did to it.

When the lawyer finally wound down from his ranting and raving, the officer shook his head in disgust and disbelief, "I can't believe how materialistic you lawyers are," he said. "You are so focused on your possessions that you don't notice anything else." "How can you say such a thing?" Asked the lawyer. The cop replied, "Don't you know that your left arm is missing from the elbow down? It must have been torn off when the truck hit you." "What!" screamed the lawyer, My Rolex is gone!"

TIMES HAVE CERTAINLY CHANGED

Over five thousand years ago, Moses said to the children of Isreal, "Pick up your shovels, mount your asses and camels and I will lead you to the Promised Land. Nearly 75 years ago (when Welfare was first introduced), President Roosevelt said, "Lay down your shovels, sit on your asses, and light up a Camel, this is the Promised Land!"

THE BODY PARTS MEETING

THE COLONSCOPY - All the organs of the body were having a meeting trying to decide who was the one in charge.

THE BRAIN - I should be in charge because, "I run all the body's system, so without me, nothing would happen."

THE BLOOD - I should be in charge, said the blood, "Because I circulate oxygen all over so without me, you'd all waste away."

THE STOMACH - I should be in charge," said the stomach, "Because I process food and give all of you energy."

THE LEGS - I should be in charge said the legs, "Because I carry the body wherever it needs to go."

THE EYES - I should be in charge, said the eyes, "Because I allow the body to see where it goes."

THE RECTUM - I should be in charge, said the rectum, "Because I'm responsible for waste removable."

All the other body parts laughed at the rectum and insulted him, so in a huff, he shut down tight. Within a few days, the brain had a terrible headache, the stomach was bloated, the legs got wobbly, the Eyes got watery, and the blood was toxic. They all decided that the rectum should be the boss. The Moral of the Story? The A-hole is usually the one in charge.

THE MARRIAGE

Paula, a mother was anxiously awaiting her daughter Janet's plane to land. Janet had just come back from abroad trying to find adventure during her gap year. As Janet was exiting the plane, Paula noticed a man directly behind her daughter dressed in feathers with exotic markings all over his body, carrying a shrunken head. Janet introduced this man as her new husband. Paula gasped out loud in disbelief and disappointment and screamed, "I said for you to marry a rich doctor. A RICH DOCTOR!"

LOVE MUM EY?

Brenda and Terry are going out for the evening. The last thing they do is put their cat out. The taxi arrives, and as the couple walk out of the house, the cat scoots back in. Terry returns inside to case it out. Brenda, not wanting it known that the house would be empty, explains to the taxi driver, "My husband is just going upstairs to say goodbye to Mummie. He'll be a moment.

Several minutes later, the exhausted husband climbs back into the taxi saying, "Sorry I took so long, the stupid idiot was hiding under the bed and I had to poke her with a coat hanger several times before I could get her to come out!

THOUGHT FOR THE DAY

I don't mind coming to work, but it's the eight hour wait to go home that kills me!

THOSE LAWYERS AGAIN

Two lawyers arrive at the pub and ordered a couple of drinks. They then take sandwiches from their briefcases and began to eat. Seeing this, the angry publican approaches them and says, "Excuse me, but you cannot eat your own sandwiches in here!" The two hunched their shoulders, grunted and switched sandwiches.

LAWYER JOKES

What's the difference between a female lawyer and a pit bull? Lipstick.

A man walked into a lawyer's office and inquired about the lawyer's rates. "$50 for three questions," replied the lawyer. "Isn't that awfully steep?" Asked the man. "Yes," the lawyer replied. "And what was your third question?"

LAWYER'S CREED: A man is innocent until proven broke.

A lawyer was walking down the street and saw an auto accident. He rushed over, started handing out business cards and says, "I saw the whole thing. I'll take either side."

What is the difference between a lawyer and a herd of buffalo? The lawyer charges more.

Why won't sharks attack lawyers? Professional courtesy.

SOUNDS LIKE MRS. JONES IS IN CHARGE HERE!

Trial. A small town prosecuting attorney called his first witness to the stand in a trial, a grandmotherly, elderly woman. He approached her and asked, "Mrs. Jones, do you know me?"

She responded, "Why yes, I do know you Mr. Williams. I've known you since you were a young boy. And frankly, you've been a big disappointment to me. You lie, you cheat on your wife, and you manipulate people and talk about them behind their backs. You think you're a rising big shot when you haven't the brains to realize you never will amount to anything more than a two bit paper pusher. Yes, I know you."

The lawyer was stunned. Not knowing what else to do he pointed across the room and asked, "Mrs. Williams, do you know the defense attorney?"

She again replied, "Why, yes I do. I've known Mr. Bradley since he was a youngster, too. I used to babysit him for his parents. And he, too, has been a real disappointment to me. He's lazy, bigoted, he has a drinking problem.

That man can't build a normal relationship with anyone and his law practice is one of the shoddiest in the entire state. Yes, I know him."

At that point the judge rapped the courtroom to silence and called both counselors to the bench. In a very quiet voice, he said with menace, "If either of you asks her if she knows me, you'll be jailed for contempt!"

FORGET ABOUT IT!

The Dalai lama visited the White House and told the President that he could teach him to find a higher state of consciousness. then after talking to Bush for a few minutes, he said: You know what? Let's just grab lunch.

Bill Maher

CIGARS FOR THE JUDGE

A defendant in a lawsuit involving large sums of money was talking to his lawyers. "If I lose this case, I'll be ruined." "It's in the judge's hands now," said the lawyer. "Would it help if I sent the judge a box or cigars?" "Oh no! This judge is a stickler for ethical behavior. A stunt like that would prejudice him against you. He might even hold you in contempt of court. In fact you shouldn't even smile at the judge."

Within the course of time, the judge rendered a decision in favor of the defendant. As the defendant left the courthouse, he said to his lawyer, "thanks for the tip about the cigars. It worked!" "I'm sure we would have lost the case if you'd sent them." "But I did send them." "What? You did?" said the lawyer, incredulously. "Yes. That's how we won the case." "I don't understand," said the lawyer. "It's easy. I sent the cigars to judge, but signed the Plaintiff's name."

GUESS WHO?

A guy walks into a post office one day to see a middle-aged balding man standing at the counter methodically placing "Love" stamps on bright pink envelopes with hearts all over them. He then takes out a perfume bottle and starts spraying scent all over them.

His curiosity getting the better of him, he goes up to the balding man and asks what he is doing. The man says, "I'm sending out 1,000 Valentine cards signed, "Guess who?" "But why?" asks the man. "I'm a divorce lawyer," the man replies.

FUNERAL NOTICE

Sad News to Report...

Please join me in remembering a great icon of the entertainment community. The Pillsbury doughboy died yesterday of a yeast infection and trauma complication from repeated pokes in the belly. He was 71 and rolling in dough. Doughboy was buried in a lightly greased coffin.

Dozens of celebrities turned out to pay their respects, including Mrs. Butterworth, Hungry Jack, the California Raisins, Betty Crocker, the Hostess Twinkies and Captain Crunch. The grave was piled high with flours.

Aunt Jemima delivered the eulogy and lovingly described Doughboy as a man who never knew how much he was kneaded. Born and bread in Minnesota, Doughboy rose quickly in show business. But his later life was filled with turnovers. He was not considered a very smart cookie, wasting much of his dough on half-baked schemes. Despite being a little flaky at times, he still was a crusty old man and was considered a positive roll model for millions.

Doughboy is survived by his wife, Play Dough, three children, John Dough and Dosey Dough, plus they had one in the oven. He is also survived by his elderly father Pop Tart. The funeral was held at 3:30 for about 25 minutes.

POLISH SCIENTIFIC PLANS

Poland sent its top team of scientists to attend the International Science Convention, where all the countries of the world gathered to compare their scientific achievements and plans. The scientists listened to the United States describe how they were another step closer to a cure for cancer, and the Russians were preparing a space ship to go to Saturn, and Germany was inventing a car that runs on water. Soon it was the Polish scientists' turn to speak. "We are preparing a space ship to fly to the sun. This of course was met with much ridicule. They were asked how they planned to deal with the sun's extreme heat. "Simple. We're going at night!"

IT'S NOT A GOOD TIME TO BE AN ANT

Every day, a small ant arrives at work very early and starts work immediately. She produces a lot and she was happy. The Chief, a lion, was surprised to see that the ant was working without supervision.

The chief thought if the ant can produce so much without supervision, wouldn't she produce even more if she had a supervisor. So he recruited a cockroach who had extensive experience as a supervisor and who was famous for writing excellent reports. The cockroach's first decision was to set up a clocking in attendance system. He also needed a secretary to help him write and type his reports and he recruited a spider, who managed the archives and monitored all phone calls.

The owl spent three months in the department and came up with an enormous report, in several volumes, that concluded: The department is overstaffed. Guess who the lion fired first?

The ant, of course, because she showed lack of motivation and had a negative attitude. It's not a good time to be an ant.

DOUBLE VISION IS THE KEY

A businessman enters a tavern, sits down at the bar, and orders a double martini on the rocks. After he finishes the drink, he peeks inside his shirt pocket, and then orders another double martini. After he finishes that, he again peeks inside his shirt pocket and orders another one.

The bartender says: "Look, buddy, I've been bringing you martinis all night long - but you got to tell me why you look inside your shirt pocket before you order a refill." The customer replies: "I'm peeking at a photo of my wife. When she starts to look good, I know it's time to go home!"

SUBJECT: HOW BAD IS THE ECONOMY?

The economy is so bad...

Jury duty is now considered a good-paying job.

African TV is now showing, Sponsor an American Child commercials.

I ordered a burger at McDonalds and the kid behind the counter asked, "Can you afford fries with that?"

CEO's are now playing miniature golf.

Exxon-Mobil laid off 25 Congressmen

My ATM gave me an IOU!

A stripper was killed when her audience showered her with rolls of pennies while she danced.

I saw a Mormon polygamist with only one wife.

I bought a toaster oven and my free gift with a purchase was a bank.

If the bank returns your check marked, "insufficient funds" you have to call them and ask if they meant you or them.

Angelina Jolie adopted a child from America.

Parents in Beverly Hills fired their nannies and learned the names of their children.

My cousin had an exorcism but couldn't afford to pay for it, and they repossessed her.

A truckload of Americans was caught sneaking into Mexico.

Motel Six won't leave the light on for you anymore.

A picture is now worth only 200 words.

They renamed Wall Street "Wal-Mart Street.

When Bill and Hillary travel together, they now have to share a room.

One of the casinos in Las Vegas is now managed by Somali pirates.

And finally, I was so depressed last night thinking about the economy, wars, jobs, my savings, social security, retirement funds, etc. I called the Suicide Hotline. I got a call center in Pakistan, and when I told them I was suicidal, they got all excited and asked if I could drive a truck.

VIAGRA INGREDIENTS REVEALED

After much research and millions of dollars, our scientists have discovered the secret ingredients to Viagra.

Top Secret

Vitamin E......3%

Aspirin...........2%

Ibuprofen.......1%

Vitamin C.......1%

Fix-A-Flat.......92%

HELP FROM ABOVE

As I was driving home one day, worrying about all of the chaos in Washington, and how my life was falling apart, I saw a yard sign that said:

NEED HELP??? CALL JESUS 1-800-555-1223

Out of sheer desperation and curiosity, I called the number. The next day, a little old man of Mexican descent shuffled up my walkway, dragging an equally old lawn mower.

Note: There is a job out there for everyone who wants one.

PSYCHIATRISTS VS. BARTENDERS

Ever since I was a child, I've always had a fear that something was under my bed at night. So I went to a shrink and told him. "I've got problems. Every time I go to bed I think there's somebody under it. I'm going crazy!" "Just put yourself in my hands for one year," said the shrink. "Come talk to me in a week and we should be able to get rid of those fears."

"How much do you charge?" I asked. "Eighty dollars per visit," the doctor replied. "I'll sleep on it," I said. Six months later the doctor met me on the street. "Why didn't you come to see me about those fears you were having?" he asked.

"Well, eighty bucks a visit, three times a week, for a year is an awful lot of money! A bartender cured me for $10, I was so happy to have saved all that money that I went and bought a new pick-up truck." "What was his advice?" the shrink asked. "He told me to cut the legs off my bed."

WHIMSICAL WIZARD SAYS:

- It's not whether you win or lose, but how you place the blame.

- You are not drunk if you can lie on the floor without holding on.

- We have enough youth. How about a fountain of "smart"?

- The original point and click interface was a Smith and Wesson.

- A fool and his money can throw one heck of a party.

- When blondes have more fun do they know it?

- Five days a week my body is a temple. The other two is an amusement park.

- Learn from your parents' mistakes. Use birth control.

CHAPTER V

SIZZLING SENIORS

In this chapter, the LAUGHMAKERS are the wise, witty and hysterically worldly senior citizens. So, loosen your collar, take off your girdle, flop down in your easy chair and forget the challenges of the day. Let's take an entertaining tour through the side-splitting humor found in the Center for Sizzling Seniors.

GRANNIE'S VISIT

"Oh grannie, I sure am glad to see you. Now Dad will do the trick he's been promising us." The grandmother said, "What trick is that Billy?" "He told Mommy that he'd climb the walls if you came to visit."

OOPS! BE CAREFUL FOR WHAT YOU WISH FOR

A married couple in their early 60's was celebrating their 40th wedding anniversary in a quiet, romantic little restaurant. Suddenly, a tiny, yet beautiful fairy appeared on their table. She said, "For being such an exemplary married couple and for being loving to each other for all this time, I will grant you each a wish." The wife answered, "Oh, I want to travel around the world with my darling husband. The fairy waved her magic wand and poof! Two tickets for the Queen Mary II appeared in her hands.

The husband thought for a moment. "Well, this is all very romantic, but an opportunity like this will never come again.

I'm sorry, my love, but my wish is to have a wife 30 years younger than me." The wife and the fairy were deeply disappointed, but a wish is a wish. So the fairy waved her magic wand and poof! The husband became 92 years old. the moral of the story: Men who are ungrateful should remember that fairies are female.

A little old man shuffled into an ice cream parlor and pulled himself slowly, painfully, up onto a stool. After catching his breath, he ordered a banana split. The waitress asked kindly, "Crushed nuts, sir?" "No," he replied, "arthritis."

SENIOR DRESS CODE

Many folks over 50 are quite confused today about how they should present themselves. Feeling young, they try to conform to current fashions and present a youthful image. Contrary to what you may have seen on the streets, the following combinations DO NOT go together and should be avoided:

- A nose ring and bifocals
- Spiked hair and bald spots
- A pierced tongue and dentures
- Miniskirts and support hose
- Ankle bracelets and corn pads
- Speedos and cellulite
- A belly button ring and a gall bladder surgery scar
- Unbuttoned shirts and a heart monitor
- Midriff shirts and a midriff bulge
- Bikinis and liver spots
- Miniskirts and varicose veins
- And most importantly...

At some point you have to give up the "Daisy Duke" shorts.

MIRACLE NEEDED

A scientist and a philosopher were being chased by a hungry lion. After the scientist made some quick calculations, he said, "It's no good trying to outrun it, it's catching up." The philosopher kept a little ahead and replied, "I am not trying to outrun the lion. I am trying to outrun you!"

NEW COWBOY BOOTS

An elderly couple, Margaret and Bert, moved to Texas. Bert had always wanted a pair of authentic cowboy boots, so on seeing some for sale; he bought them and wore them home. Walking proudly, he sauntered into the kitchen and said to his wife, "Notice anything different about me?" Margaret looked him over. "Nope."

Frustrated, Bert stormed off into the bathroom, undressed and walked back into the kitchen completely naked except for the boots. Again he asked Margaret, a little louder this time, "Notice anything different NOW?"

Margaret looked up and said in her best deadpan, "Bert, what's different? It's hanging down today, it was hanging down yesterday and it'll be hanging down again tomorrow."

Furious, Bert yelled, "AND DO YOU KNOW WHY IT'S HANGING DOWN, MARGARET?" "Nope, not a clue." she replied.

Now even more furious, Bert yelled, "IT'S HANGING DOWN, BECAUSE IT'S LOOKING AT MY NEW BOOTS!" Without missing a beat Margaret replied, "Shoulda bought a hat, Bert, shoulda bought a hat."

SENIOR WEDDING PLANS

Jacob, age 92, and Rebecca, age 89, living in Miami, are all excited about their decision to get married. They go for a stroll to discuss the wedding, and on the way they pass a drugstore. Jacob suggests they go in.

Jacob addresses the man behind the counter:

"Are you the owner?"

The pharmacist answers, "Yes."

Jacob: "We're about to get married. Do you sell heart medication?"

Pharmacist: "Of course we do."

Jacob: "How about medicine for circulation?"

Pharmacist: "All kinds."

Jacob: "Medicine for rheumatism?"

Pharmacist: "Definitely."

Jacob: "How about suppositories?"

Pharmacist: "You bet!"

Jacob: "Medicine for memory problems, arthritis and Alzheimer's?"

Pharmacist: "Yes, a large variety. The works."

Jacob: "What about vitamins, sleeping pills, Geritol, antidotes for Parkinson's disease?"

Pharmacist: "Absolutely."

Jacob: "Everything for heartburn and indigestion?"

Pharmacist: "We sure do."

Jacob: "You sell wheelchairs and walkers and canes?"

Pharmacist: "All speeds and sizes."

Jacob: "Adult diapers?"

Pharmacist: "Sure."

Jacob: "We'd like to use this store as our Bridal Registry".

HOW TO TRAIN A PARROT

A man buys a pet parrot and brings him home. But the parrot starts insulting him and gets really nasty, so the man picks up the parrot and tosses him into the freezer to teach him a lesson. He hears the bird squawking for a few minutes, but all of a sudden the parrot is quiet. The man open the freezer door, the parrot walks out, looks up at him and says, "I apologize for offending you, and I humbly ask your forgiveness." The man says, "Well, thank you. You are forgiven. The parrot then says, "Sir, if you don't mind my asking, what did that chicken do?"

HARD OF HEARING

An old man decided his old wife was getting hard of hearing. So, he called her doctor to make an appointment to have her hearing checked. The doctor said he could see her in two weeks and meanwhile, there's a simple, informal test the husband could do to give the doctor some idea of the dimensions of the problem. "Here's what you do. Start about 40 feet away from her, and speak in a normal conversational tone and see if she hears you. If not, go to 30 feet, then 20 feet and so on until you get a response."

That evening, she's in the kitchen cooking dinner, and he's in the living room, and he says to himself, "I'm about 40 feet away, let's see what happens. "Honey, what's for supper?" So he moves to the other end of the room, about 30 feet and asks again. "Honey what's for dinner?" No response. This happened at 20 and 10 feet. Still no response. So he walks right up behind her and says again, "Honey, what's for supper?" FOR THE FIFTH TIME, CHICKEN DEAR!"

WHAT PART OF THE GOLDEN RULE IS THIS?

This letter was sent to the Principals office after the school had sponsored a luncheon for the elderly. An elderly lady received a new radio at the lunch as a door prize and was writing to say thank you.

Dear Kean Elementary:

God bless you for the beautiful radio I won at your recent senior citizens luncheon. I am 84 years old and live at the Sprenger Home for the Aged. All of my family has passed away. I am all alone now and it's nice to know that someone is thinking of me. God bless you for your kindness to an old forgotten lady. My roommate is 95 and has always had her own radio; she would never let me listen to hers, even when she was napping.

The other day her radio fell off the night stand and broke into a lot of pieces. It was awful and she was in tears.

Her distress over the broken radio touched me and I knew winning this radio was God's way of answering my prayers. She asked if she could listen to mine, and I told her to kiss my ___.

Thank you for that opportunity.

Sincerely,

Agnes Baker

A RULE FOR THANKSGIVING AT TANEKA'S HOUSE

Don't get in line asking questions about the food. Who made the potato salad? Is there egg in it? Are the greens fresh? Is the meat in the greens turkey or pork? Who made the macaroni and cheese? What kind of pie is that? Who made it? Ask one more question, Taneka said, and I will punch you in your mouth, knocking out all your fronts so you won't be able to eat nothin!

Jonathan Slocomb, popular host of BET-TV's Comic View, told this amusing joke.

An elderly lady came home from church one Sunday and found a man robbing her home. She screams, "Stop!" and quoted a scripture she remembered the minister quoted in his sermon. The robber froze. And the lady ran to the phone and called the police. Because they knew her two officers got to her house in a matter of minutes and handcuffed the crook. As they were taking him out of the house, one of the policemen asked the robber why he was rigidly standing until they arrived. The guy answered, "She screamed at me and said stop. I got an ax and two 38's. The old lady said, "I did not say that. I said Acts 2:38

YOU'RE WHO"?

A middle-aged woman had a heart attack and was rushed to the hospital. On her way there, she slipped into a coma and found herself in front of the pearly gates. She asked St. Peter if this was her time, but Peter scanned his book and said no she had another 35 years to live.

Elated, the woman woke up, received treatment and was released after a short stay in the hospital.

She decided that since she had another 35 years ahead of her, she would make some changes that she had always wanted to make. Off she went to the cosmetic doctor and had a face-lift, a nose job, a tummy tuck, had her hair dyed and bought an entire new wardrobe.

After a few days of rest, she got dressed up looking like a million dollars and walked out of the house. Then as she was crossing the street, the lady was struck by a car and was killed.

Back in front of St. Peter, she said, "St. Peter, you told me I had another 35 years to live! ""Oh my mistake," St. Peter said. "I am so sorry. But you see, I didn't recognize you."

OLD IS WHEN...

Your sweetie says, "Let's go upstairs and make love,' and you answer, 'Pick one. I can't do both!"

Your friends compliment you on your new alligator shoes and you're barefoot.

Going bra-less pulls all the wrinkles out of your face.

You don't care where your spouse goes, just as long as you don't have to go along.

You are cautioned to slow down by the doctor instead of by the police.

Getting a little action means you don't need to take a laxative today.

Getting lucky means you find your car in the parking lot.

An all-nighter means not getting up to use the bathroom.

You're not sure if these are facts or jokes.

YES YOU CAN!

Success in life does not consist of who you become or what you acquire, but rather who others become because of your presence.

Never underestimate the power of your actions. With one small gesture you can change a person's life - for better or for worse.

KEEP THE MOTOR RUNNING

The marriage of an 80 year old man and a 20 year old woman was the talk of the town. After being married a year, the couple went to the hospital for the birth of their first child. The attending nurse came out of the delivery room to congratulate the old gentleman and said, "This is amazing. How do you do it at your age?" The old man grinned and said, "You got to keep the old motor running."

The following year, the couple returned to the hospital for the birth of their second child. The same nurse was attending the delivery and again went out to congratulate the old gentleman. She said, "Sir, you are something else. How do you manage it?" The old man grinned and said, "You gotta keep the old motor running."

A year later, the couple returned to the hospital for the birth of their third child. The same nurse was there for this birth also and, after the delivery, she once again approached the old gentleman, smiled, and said, "Well, you surely are something else! How do you do it?" The old man replied, "It's like I've told you before, you gotta keep the old motor running." The nurse, still smiling, patted him on the back and said, "Well, I guess it's time to change the oil. This one's black."

THE PARKING TICKETS

Working people frequently ask retired people what they do to make their days interesting. Here's an example. The other day, my wife, Bev, and I went into town and visited a shop. When we came out, there was a cop writing out a parking ticket.

We went up to him and I said, "Come on, man. How about giving a senior citizen a break?" He ignored us and continued writing the ticket. I called him an a_ _ hole.

He glared at me and started writing another ticket for having worn out tires.

Then I called him a butt head. He finished the second ticket and put it on the windshield with the first. Then he started writing more tickets. This went on for about 20 minutes. The more we abused him, the more tickets he wrote. Just then, our bus arrived, and we got on it and went home.

We try to have a little fun each day now that we're retired. It's important at our age.

SNATCH AND GRAB

A senior citizen's group charters an overnight gambling casino bus trip from Tampa, Florida to Branson, MO. As they entered Missouri, an elderly woman comes up to the bus driver and says, "I've just been molested." The driver felt that she had fallen asleep and had a dream so he tells her to go back to her seat, and sit down. A short time later, another old woman comes forward, and claims that she was just been molested.

The driver thought he had a bus load of old wackos, and who would be molesting those old ladies anyhow. About ten minutes later, a third old lady comes up and say that she'd also been molested.

The bus driver decided that he's had enough of this, and pulls into the first rest area. When he turns the lights on and stands up, he sees and old man on his hands and knees crawling in the aisles. "Hey Gramps, what are you doing down there?" Says the driver. "I've lost my toupee. I thought I found it three times, but every time I tried to grab it runs away."

ONCE A FISHERMAN ALWAYS...

An elderly couple was on a cruise and it was really very stormy. They were standing on the back of the boat watching the storm, when a wave came up and washed the old man overboard. They searched for days and couldn't find the body. The captain sent the old woman back to shore with the promise that he would notify her as soon as they found something.

Three weeks went by and finally the old woman got a fax from the boat. It read, Ma'am, sorry to inform you, we found your husband dead at the bottom of the ocean. We hauled him up to the deck and attached to his butt was an oyster and in it was a pearl worth $50,000. Please advise.

The old woman faxed back: "Send me the pearl, and re-bait the trap."

ONCE, TWICE-BUT NOT THREE TIMES A LADY

A funeral service was being held for a woman who had just passed away. At the end of the service, the pallbearers were carrying the casket out when they accidentally bumped into a wall, jarring the casket. They heard a faint moan. They opened the casket and found that the woman was actually alive. She lived for ten more years, and then died. Once again, a ceremony was held, and at the end of it, the pallbearers were carrying out the casket. As they proceeded towards the door, the husband cried out, "Watch that wall!"

YOU KNOW YOU ARE TOO OLD TO TRICK OR TREAT WHEN:

You get winded from knocking on the door

You have to have another kid chew the candy for you.

You ask for high fiber candy only.

When someone drops a candy bar in your bag, you lose balance and fall over.

People say, "Great Boris Karloff Mask" and you're not wearing a mask.

When the door opens and you yell, "Trick or ..." and you can't remember the rest.

By the end of the night you have a bag full of restraining orders

You have to carefully choose a costume that won't dislodge your hairpiece

You're the only Power Ranger in the neighborhood with a walker.

And the number one reason Seniors should not go Trick or Treating is because you keep having to go home to pee.

Oh well. Have a happy Halloween anyway.

> *"Older people shouldn't eat health food, they need all the preservatives they can get."*
>
> *Robert Orben*

A single glass at night could mean a peaceful, uninterrupted night's sleep.

NEW WINE FOR SENIORS

California vintners in the Napa Valley area, which primarily produce Pinot Blanc, Pinot Noir, and Pinot Grigio wines, have developed a new hybrid grape that acts as an anti-diuretic. It is expected to reduce the number of trips older people have to make to the bathroom during the night.

The new wine will be marketed as Pino More.

TOGETHER AGAIN

A man left for a holiday to Jamaica. His wife was on a business trip and was planning to meet him the next day. When he reached his hotel, he decided to send her an email. Unable to find the scrap of paper on which he had written her web address, so he did his best to type from memory. Unfortunately he missed one letter, and his note went to an elderly preacher's wife whose husband had passed away only one day before. When the grieving widow checked her email, she let out a piercing scream and fell to the floor dead. Her family rushed into the room and saw this note on the screen: Dearest wife just got checked in. Everything prepared for your arrival tomorrow. Your loving husband.

P.S. Sure is hot down here.

AND HERE IS ONE LAST LAUGH

A mature lady gets pulled over for speeding.

Lady: Is there a problem officer?

Cop: Yes ma'am, I'm afraid you were speeding.

Lady: Oh, I see.

Cop: Can I see your license please?

Lady: Well, I would give it to you, but I don't have one.

Cop: Don't have one?

Lady: No. I lost it 4 years ago for drunk driving.

Cop: Can I see your vehicle registration papers please.

Lady: I can't do that.

Cop: Why not?

Lady: I stole this car.

Cop: Stole it?

Lady: Yes, and I killed and hacked up the owner.

Cop: You what?

Lady: His body parts are in plastic bags in the trunk if you want to see.

The traffic cop looks at the woman and slowly backs away to his car while calling for back up. Within minutes 5 police cars circle the car. A senior officer slowly approaches the car, clasping his half-drawn gun.

Cop Two: Ma'am, could you step out of your vehicle please! The woman steps out of her vehicle.

Lady: Is there a problem sir?

Cop Two: My colleague here tells me that you have stolen this car and murdered the owner.

Lady: Murdered the owner? Are you serious?

Cop Two: Yes, could you please open the trunk of your car, please. The woman opens the trunk, revealing nothing but an empty trunk.

Cop Two: Is this your car, ma'am?

Lady: Yes, here are the registration papers. The traffic cop was stunned.

Cop Two: My colleague claims that you do not have a driving license. The woman digs into her handbag and pulls out a clutch purse and hands it to the officer. The officer examines the license quizzically.

Cop Two: Thank you ma'am, but I am puzzled, as I was told by my officer here that you didn't have a license, that you stole this car, and that you murdered and hacked up the owner!

Lady: Bet he also told you I was speeding too!

Don't mess with seniors, they can out think ya!!!

HATE TO SAY GOODBYE

Each day, remember to say thank you for:
God's power to guide me
God's might to uphold me
God's wisdom to teach me
God's eye to watch over me
God's ear to hear me
God's word to give me speech
God's hand to guide me
God's way to lie before me
God's shield to shelter me
God's host to secure me and remember
God Loves You Too, Inc. (GLU2)

May love and laughter light your days and warm your heart and home. May good and faithful friends be yours wherever you may roam.

Stay Inspired.

Thelma Shirley–Taylor

ORDER MORE COPIES TODAY

If you wish to order additional copies of this book, (For gifts to loved ones, friends, church members or business colleagues) you may do so by mail, phone or the internet;

Name:_____

Address:_____

City/State:_____ Zip:_____

Phone:_____

Email: _____

Number of Books: _____ @19.95 each, (check our website for bulk order discounts)

Make all checks payable to: THTH, Inc. ("The Ha That Heals" or Thelma Shirley-Taylor)

Visit our website at: www.thehathatheals.com

Email us at: laughagain@thehathatheals.com

Call us at: (708) 357-7141

Contact us by mail at: THTH, INC.
4710 Lincoln Hwy, Suite 180, Matteson, IL. 60443

SPEAKERS PUBLISHERS & AUTHORS ASSOCIATION

If you are interested in becoming a paid professional speaker, or wish to finally publish that book you have been talking about for years, you need to join **SPAA** today! We are dedicated to providing you with the most comprehensive and interactive training currently available, visit us online at **www.thespaa.org**, or call us at **1-866-990-6772**.